loving your body

FOCUS ON THE FAMILY®

Dr. Deborah Newman

loving your body

*Embracing Your
True Beauty
in Christ*

TYNDALE

Tyndale House Publishers, Inc.
Wheaton, Illinois

Loving Your Body
Copyright © 2002 by Deborah Newman
All rights reserved. International copyright secured.

ISBN: 1-58997-005-5

A Focus on the Family book published by
Tyndale House Publishers, Wheaton, Illinois 60189
Renewing the Heart is a registered trademark of Focus on the Family.

The case examples presented in this book are fictional composites based on the author's clinical experience with hundreds of clients through the years. Any resemblance between these fictional characters and actual persons is coincidental.

Library of Congress Cataloging-in-Publication Data

Newman, Deborah.
   Loving your body : embracing your true beauty in Christ / Deborah Newman.
      187 p. , 23 cm.
Includes bibliographical references.
   ISBN: 1-58997-005-5
   1. Christian women—Religious life. 2. Body image in women—Religious aspects—Christianity. 3. Self-acceptance in women—Religious aspects—Christianity. I. Title.
   BV4527 .N455 2002
   248.8/43 21

                                    2001005647

Edited by: Kathy Davis and Liz Duckworth
Front Cover Design: Lovgren Marketing Group
Interior Design: Angela Barnes

Printed in the United States of America
3 4 5 6 7 8 9 / 08 07 06 05 04 03

To my favorite daughter, Rachel.
You are beautiful—
mind, body, and soul.

Contents

Acknowledgments

This is a book I needed to write, not one I wanted to write. I wrote it with a passion in my heart for the many women and girls who are being seduced by the lies of Satan. My heart is concerned for our daughters because they are at greater risk of body despair in our present times than in any other. I pray that it will be a life-changing tool, that it will equip readers with the Truth of God's Word.

From the beginning, the Focus on the Family creative writing team and Renewing the Heart Women's Ministry have partnered with me in accomplishing this task. I'm grateful to the many people who work behind the scenes at Focus on the Family, especially Mark Maddox, Kathy Davis, Julie Küss, Liz Duckworth, and Mary Houser.

Thank you to the Park Cities Baptist Church Prayer Committee, Esther Department, Horn Department, TCA Prayer Moms, and so many others who lifted me and this project up in prayer.

My husband, Brian, was my silent partner supplying research assistance, encouragement, grocery shopping, carpooling, and anything else that was needed. You're the greatest! I'm so blessed to have two wonderful and understanding children, Rachel and Ben. Thanks for doing your part.

I'm grateful that God has allowed me this wonderful privilege to minister to women. "For it is God who is at work in you, both to will and to work for *His* good pleasure" (Philippians 2:13, NASB).

Introduction: An Invitation to Freedom

Marybeth was asked to be a model in the fashion show her church's women's ministry was sponsoring to raise money for their spring retreat. Her answer was typical for Marybeth: "I couldn't do that." She said it sweetly and seemed so humble. No one would have suspected that at age 49, as a grandmother-to-be with two grown daughters, Marybeth was one of the most insecure women around. Although she dressed attractively and looked her best, deep inside she harbored a tremendous vault filled with body hate that bordered on disgust. Beneath her quick reply, "I couldn't do that," lay this painful thought: "How could you even suggest such a thing! The last thing I would do is walk onto a stage inviting people to look at me. I don't need anyone else to look at every bulge or inspect my latest wrinkle. Believe me, I can do that all by myself."

Marybeth's dilemma is made all the more significant by the fact that Christine, who took her place, was a 38-year-old, overweight mother of three who was honored to be asked. She thought nothing of walking her size 18 body down the runway of the church. She enjoyed every minute of it. Christine knows that she needs to lose weight and has recently started a workout program, but just because she doesn't have the perfect body doesn't mean she's not comfortable in it—especially in the company of her friends.

I've struggled all my life to accept
myself because of my weight.

Marybeth's and Christine's differences in body perspectives came to mind recently as I sat in my counseling office across from Susan. She's an attractive 16 year old. She's not being pursued by top modeling agencies, but she's above average in appearance. She has thick, naturally blond hair with a slight wave. She's 5'4" and she wears a size nine. She's on the drill team at school and takes dance lessons twice a week so she can keep ahead of the competition for her coveted spot. So why is she in my counseling office? Because she is depressed, which she admits to her mom, but she is also in the first stages of bulimia, which she will barely admit to herself.

As Susan tells me about her life and her problem with depression, I'm getting a little angry inside. I'm not angry at Susan. I'm angry about the outrageous pressure to look perfect that Susan faces every day. I'm mad because a wonderful creation of God stares at herself in Lycra 10 to 12 hours a week and cringes at her appearance. It struck me a little more poignantly as I listened to Susan describe her body. She told me that her only positive physical characteristic is her big brown eyes. What she hates most about herself is her height and her midsection. She wants to be six feet tall, and she thinks she can stand to lose a few pounds and thin out through her stomach, hips, and thighs. I've heard all that before, but what really got to me this time was the way she talked about her arms. She complained that she hates the way her flabby arms wave in the wind!

For almost two decades as a Christian counselor, I've listened to girls and women describe their body hate. They've mainly focused on their hips, stomach, thighs, and breasts. In the same week I met with Susan, I had heard three different females, one 40 year old, another teenager, and now Susan, complaining about their arms! When is it going to stop?

I despise hearing this same painful story repeated over and over. It begins as predictably as, "Once upon a time," except there is no "happily ever after." There's something about her body that she doesn't like. It doesn't quite fit with her perception of what's beautiful. Whether she is too short, her thighs are too big, her breasts are too small or too saggy, a woman's body hate can lead to depression, eating disorders, and unneeded surgery. This kind of preoccupation with her appearance can even be fatal through suicide, botched surgery, or deadly complications from eating disorders. It is a serious problem.

The teenage years have always been a period of preoccupation with looks. This fixation is even more serious in the twenty-first century. But it is no longer confined to the teen and young adult years. Some women, like Marybeth, struggle with an unhealthy obsession about their looks all their lives. We can't ignore this problem that is wreaking havoc in the lives of girls, teenagers, and women.

It's difficult to have problems with
vision and hearing as I get older.

I've got to help fight the body-hating insanity I find all around me. I can help one person at a time in my counseling office, but I feel compelled to do more—to sound a warning, to challenge women and girls to get together and talk about the problem, to confront the lies, and to support one another in living in the truth. My hope is to help mothers consider this issue in their lives so they are able to help their daughters live in dignity, not self-imposed disgrace. I long for women in the church to reveal to a confused and mixed-up world how God's love, purpose, and acceptance transcend cultural pressure to look good!

That's why I've written this book. That's why I'm glad you are joining with me in fighting for truth, first within yourself, and then by teaching others. Together we can take a stand against negative body stress! In my years of experience I have witnessed how God's Word, taught in the context of supportive relationships, dramatically transforms lives. I think the Marybeths, Christines, and Susans need to sit down and talk together. They need to study God's Word and discover the truth about their bodies. They need to stop the epidemic of body hate and keep it from devastating their own and others' lives.

I am thrilled that you are reading this book. I can't wait for you to learn the joy of liking the body you live in. I doubt that you are even aware of how much a negative body image can affect you. God has so much He wants to show you about the meaning of your life and His perspective on your body. In the culture we live in, I believe it is critical for women to think about this subject.

---

*Breast cancer has changed almost every part of my
body for the worse: My skin is dry, my hair is thinner,
my breasts aren't real. But it has also helped me focus
on what is really important, and it isn't all that other stuff.*

This is a good book for you to read on your own, but I have purposefully written it to be experienced with a group. In my years as a Christian counselor, I have witnessed the healing power of group interaction. Women, in particular, heal through relationship and connection to other women—God designed us to need each other. I encourage you to meet together with other women to share in the discussion questions at the end of each chapter. I'll never forget the 70-year-old woman who participated in a group that I led over a one-week period. At the end of the week, she said, "In all my years as a Christian, I've never felt the love and support of God in the way I have this week through all of you." It was bittersweet to hear her say those words. I was glad she finally had that beautiful experience in the body of Christ, yet I was sad that it took 70 years before she felt that kind of love and support in Christian community.

My vision for this book is that it will be a ministry tool that will bring women together to support and encourage one another. Women's ministries groups, mothers and daughters, youth groups, and neighborhood Bible studies can use this material to guide them into God's truth about a reality we all deal with. I long to see women thinking about their bodies in light of God's Word and in the context of their relationships with other believers.

I feel that God has given me a commission similar to Isaiah's. Isaiah came to the people of Israel to proclaim the good news that their nation didn't have to remain in captivity to other nations. I am coming to women to proclaim that we don't have to remain in captivity to the message that our bodies aren't good enough. In fact, I think Isaiah 61:1–3 describes the beauty that God wants to bring to women:

> ¹The Spirit of the Sovereign Lord is on me, because the Lord has anointed me to preach good news to the poor. He has sent me to bind up the brokenhearted, to proclaim freedom for the captives and release from darkness for the prisoners, ²to proclaim the year of the Lord's favor and the day of vengeance of our God, to comfort all who mourn, ³and provide for those who grieve in Zion— to bestow on them a crown of beauty instead of ashes, the oil of gladness instead of mourning, and a garment of praise instead of a spirit of despair. They will be called oaks of righteousness, a planting of the Lord for the display of his splendor.

Isn't that what you want for yourself and the women you know? Don't you want to exchange your ashes for beauty, your mourning for gladness, your spirit of despair for a garment of praise? God wants that also! So let's get started.

How to Use this Book in a Study Group

You'll get the most out of the study group if you read the assigned chapter before you come to the meeting, but don't skip the meeting if you haven't had time to complete the chapter. You'll still gain valuable insights from the other women. I recommend that you purchase a spiral notebook or journal to record your responses to the questions that are placed throughout the text. A separate journal lets you keep your personal reflections private, so you can feel free to share this book with a friend without exposing confidential information. Many of the questions are simply insights from Scripture, but some are more personal in nature. After each question, I will suggest answers that you can use for clarification and further thought. Please take the time to answer each question.

I know how busy women are, and how hard it is to find time to read and study. I've tried to make the chapters short enough that you can read and answer the questions in under an hour. May I suggest that you try to carve out just 10 minutes a day to read and work on the questions. That way you'll be finished with the chapter before your weekly group meeting.

The worst thing about my body is the hair
I have on my face and upper lip.

The scriptures are provided in the text so that you can bring your book along into your busy life and take advantage of small blocks of time you find within your day. Women who work outside the home may want to read during their lunch breaks. Or you may want to bring your book and journal along when you take the kids to the park and study while you watch them play. God will help you discover the best time to fit this study into your life.

Of course you may choose to look up the scriptures in your own Bible so you can underline them or know where they are found. You do not need to answer the discussion questions at the end of each chapter before the meeting unless you want to. The discussion questions don't require preparation, and will most likely be the focus of your group meeting.

Following are ground rules for a successful group discussion. Your group may have additional suggestions.

1. Everything said here is confidential.
2. Everything said here is voluntary. You may pass if you don't want to give an answer.
3. There are no right answers. (Most answers aren't right or wrong; rather, they reflect your feelings or opinions. However, the Bible is the Supreme Authority.)

During the group meetings the discussion questions at the end of each chapter will be the focus of the sharing time; however, your group might sometimes wish to discuss questions from the text as well. It will be assumed that each participant read the chapter during the previous week. There's really no need for formal teaching; merely discuss what was read.

Above all, I hope that the study group will provide you with a sense of community. Women need to have deep connections with other women. The community becomes a place where the transformation from body-loathing to body-acceptance can take place. Richard Foster gave this advice for a small group he led:

> Give encouragement as often as possible;
> advice, once in a great while;
> reproof, only when absolutely necessary;
> and judgment never.[1]

That's a good credo to use in your group. The goal of the group is to support one another in the process of allowing God to transform your lives and beliefs about who you are.

There is a special kind of intimacy that develops when you pray for one another. I encourage you to close each discussion time in prayer and have weekly prayer partners or a prayer list so you can pray for each person by name.

Again, let me say how delighted I am that you are participating in this study. I pray that it will lead to a life of freedom in which you are no longer plagued by the destructive power of dislike for your body. I pray that your group and individual study will be prosperous and that your soul will soar as you focus on what is really important and special about you. Always remember that every body *is* beautiful! Please let me know of your group's success or questions by writing me at:

Deborah Newman
Focus on the Family Author Relations
8605 Explorer Drive
Colorado Springs, CO 80920

Blessings,
Deborah Newman

Discussion Questions

On page 180 in Appendix III, you'll find suggestions for get-acquainted activities to use for this session.

CHAPTER ONE

Not Liking Your Body Isn't Pretty

Maylee will never forget the day she came home from the hairdresser when she was nine years old. Her mother had wanted to curl her straight Asian hair with a perm. In the 1970s perms were not as technical as they are now, and this one totally fried Maylee's hair. The hairdresser's only recourse was to cut off all the perm, leaving Maylee with a nearly-shaved head. She caught a glimpse of herself in the mirror as she left, and all she could think about was the teasing she would endure. She looked like a pimply-faced boy. She had come to the hairdresser with hopes of looking pretty, and she left feeling like a hideous freak. She ran to the car and hid under the dashboard. Nothing her mother said made her want to come out. When they arrived home, she ran to her room, hoping that no other human being would lay eyes on her.

Maylee's mom followed her to her room and made Maylee join her at the bathroom mirror. Maylee's mom held her daughter's shoulders and forced her to stand before the mirror. She said, "Look in the mirror,

Maylee. See the beautiful girl who stands there. Look at her strong, lean body. Look at her pretty brown eyes; see her nice round face. That girl is beautiful."

Maylee opened her eyes and at first saw only her awkward haircut and her blemishes. As her mother directed her, she began to notice that she did have some beauty, if she really looked. Her mother went on to sympathize with the shame and embarrassment she felt about her haircut. She said, "I know that your hair is not what we wanted it to look like. Your hair will grow out fast. I promise that we will never try to perm it again. But in spite of your haircut, you are a beautiful girl; don't let anyone tell you anything different."

My weight bothers me each and every day;
even every minute of every day.

Maylee remembers that lesson from the mirror more than she remembers the shame and teasing she experienced while her hair grew out. You see, focusing on the truth and getting the right perspective from her mom built her self-confidence and actually helped her fight the kind of body disgrace that plagues others.

I think God would like to ask you to stand before the mirror with Him by your side. I know He would show you the beauty that is there, the beauty you overlook. He wants to acknowledge the parts of you that go unappreciated by the culture you live in. He would give you the same advice Maylee's mother gave her: He would show you that indeed you are beautiful.

What Is Body Hate all About?

For generations women have been body haters. We overemphasize how we look. We even succumb to life-threatening measures to look good. While a man may wear a hairpiece, put shoulder pads in his coat, or wear elevated shoes, women are more likely to have cosmetic surgery, starve, and throw up. Some women literally put their lives on the line for the sake of beauty. It's not just a twenty-first century problem. Think of the corsets women wore in Civil War times. And did you know that during the Elizabethan era some women would actually take a little arsenic to achieve that pale appearance that was considered beautiful at that time?

How did we get this way? Many believe that women have achieved power through the ages because of their beauty and sexual attractiveness. For example, one of the best known Egyptian queens, Cleopatra, rose to power because of her sensuality, which gave her influence over the men who ruled the world.

Though the problem of women disliking their bodies is nothing new, the number of victims is on the increase. Some say the influence of the media and its plastering of perfectly shaped and toned women in our faces 24/7 is the reason. Others say it's the outright sinful preoccupation we have with ourselves.

What we can be certain of is that negative body image is impoverishing the lives of women and girls across our nation and certain other parts of the world. Let's look at a few statistics.

- Cosmetic surgery procedures among women have increased by a dramatic 165 percent since 1992.[1]
- More than half of teenage girls are, or think they should be, on diets. They want to lose all or some of the 40 pounds that females naturally gain between eight and 14. About 3 percent of these teens go too far, becoming anorexic or bulimic.[2]
- The *Medical Journal of Psychiatry* conducted a general population study on men with eating disorders and found that 2 percent of men compared to 4.8 percent of women have anorexia and bulimia.[3]
- The average American woman is 5'4" tall and weighs 140 pounds, while the average American model is 5'11" tall and weighs 117 pounds. Most fashion models are thinner than 98 percent of American women.[4]

- Eighty percent of American women are dissatisfied with their appearance.[5]
- Athletes are six times more likely to develop eating disorders than are other women.[6]
- Eighty percent of women say that the images of women on TV and movies and in fashion magazines and advertising make them feel insecure.[7]

I doubt that you can think of 10 women among your acquaintances who would say they are very satisfied with their appearance.

The Bride of Solomon

Even the bride of Solomon had a poor body image. She laments:

> Do not stare at me because I am dark, because I am darkened by the sun. My mother's sons were angry with me and made me take care of the vineyards; my own vineyard I have neglected (Song of Songs 1:6).

🌹 How did she feel about her body?

She actually hated her dark skin. Today many Caucasians are literally dying (from skin cancer) to be tan. This raises a fundamental point about body image: Body image is more about what's in our heads than how we look on the outside. For example, I could look in the mirror and think I look great, then notice a few hours later that I had a piece of lettuce stuck between my teeth. While I had the lettuce problem I thought I looked great because my feeling about how I looked was based on subjective information—what I thought I looked like, not objective information—what I actually looked like.

Now let's look at Song of Songs 2:1.

> I am a rose of Sharon, a lily of the valleys.

🌹 How does the bride of Solomon feel about her body now? What caused the change?

We notice that the bride of Solomon had a change of body image without changing her body. By the second chapter she is literally calling herself a rose of Sharon and a lily of the valleys. Her dark skin didn't change. They didn't have bleaching techniques in those days to get skin the "right" shade. What changed was her thinking. She began to believe she was beautiful.

It helped a whole lot that she had a man in her life who thought she was absolutely amazing. Some women reading right now are in relationships with men who constantly put them down for their weight or other body flaws. If that's your situation, you will need extra support and prayers as you begin to see yourself truthfully. However, most men, like King Solomon, don't notice the body issues women get so stuck on. Most of the men in our lives would love for us to accept ourselves and be free of body loathing.

I'm afraid to let anyone see me without makeup.

The reality is that we don't base our body image on objective data. Remember Susan, the 16 year old from chapter one who hates her arms? If Susan could focus on objective data, she would have many reasons to feel attractive. At 5'4" in a size nine she is not overweight. She is well fit. She has developed muscle mass through her weekly drill-team workouts. She is an example of prime teenage fitness, even though all of that is at risk if she follows through on the self-destructive path of bulimia. The reason Susan can't look at herself and appreciate these objective realities isn't because her mirror is distorted. Her body image has little to do with how she looks on the outside, but everything to do with what she thinks and feels on the inside.

Read the objective data about Susan:

Age: 16

Height: 5'4"

Weight: 125 pounds

Size: 9

Hair: shoulder length, naturally blond with slight wave

Fitness routine: works out 10 hours a week with the dance/drill team

Would you say:

_____ she's just right

_____ she's a little too fat

_____ she needs to exercise more

_____ she overdoes the exercise, but probably looks nice anyway

_____ you can understand why she doesn't feel attractive enough because a size nine is a little big

✺ Why do you think this way?

Read the objective data about Marybeth (the woman who refused to be in the fashion show):

Age: 49

Height: 5'6"

Weight: 150

Size: 12

Hair: short, highlighted, layered

Fitness routine: swims three times a week at the Y

Would you say:

_____ she's just right

_____ she's a little too fat

_____ she needs to exercise more

_____ she overdoes exercise, but looks good anyway

_____ you can understand why she doesn't feel good about herself because size 12 is a little big

✺ Why do you think this way?

If you are participating in a discussion group, you will probably find that there are a lot of different opinions about Susan's and Marybeth's objective information. Let's think about what influenced you to develop your opinion about your own and others' bodies.

What Is Body Image?

You develop your body image slowly without stopping to think about it. As you flip through magazines, turn channels on TV, hear comments about your body from your mother, father, siblings, boyfriend or husband, coaches, and others, and compare yourself with the women around you, you are developing your body image. Subtle beliefs get into your mind such as, "My thighs shouldn't touch, my stomach must be flat, and my arms can't wag!" All these negative thoughts can lead you on a self-destructive path if you don't recognize them.

Susan can remember actually liking herself when she was in fourth grade. She was always a fast runner and one day she even beat Tim Hill in a race during PE. She loved to get a new Easter dress each year and felt pretty when she joined her family at church. She used to get so many compliments about her naturally curly hair it was embarrassing.

I wish my nose was symmetrical.

It wasn't until sixth grade that she started to worry about her body. That summer at camp, her counselor always skipped dessert and ritualistically performed 130 sit-ups every night. Susan's girlfriends at school, who had once avoided boys like the plague, now based their worth and dignity on whether guys liked them.

Susan didn't like boys the same way her friends did, but she felt pressure to have a boyfriend. When the guy she chose, Andrew, told his friend, who told her friend that he liked her back, she felt exhilarated. But when he made fun of her wobbly thighs she felt crushed. That's the first time Susan remembers disliking her body.

Marybeth had to think hard about when she had *ever* liked her body. She couldn't even remember a time. It's not because she is older and her memory is fading. She literally began hating her body when she was four years old and her stepfather started molesting her. She hated and loved the man who hurt her, but she only hated the body to which it happened. In her four-year-old mind she reasoned, "There must be something wrong with me for him to treat me this way."

You would think with that kind of body hate Marybeth would have ignored her body and never tried to look good. Actually, the opposite was true. Marybeth spent her time trying to make herself look good enough, but never succeeded in her mind. She continually kept up with the latest fashions, and although she didn't dress seductively or extravagantly, she was an expert in gaining approval for how she dressed. It's just that the approval was never accepted—it bounced right off of her.

I feel like I would lose everything—my husband,
my friends, my life—if I gained one pound.

Christine, the woman who took Marybeth's place in the fashion show, has many painful memories from her childhood about being overweight. She dreaded the change of seasons because it meant one thing—shopping for new clothes with Mom. She remembers the ridicule she felt as her mom dragged her from store to store asking if they carried half sizes. Christine started her first diet in third grade. She desperately wanted to please her mom, but she never succeeded. In fact, just last year she realized that the yo-yo diets she had been on all her life were attempts to make her mother like her.

The funny thing is that when Christine turned 30, she wore the same dress size as her mother, and her mother was pleased that they were both the same size. Still, having her mother's approval wasn't the answer to Christine's self-rejection. Christine's body image changed when she finally let God's opinion of her body be the one that mattered. The new exercise plan she is starting is the first time she has ever done anything positive for her body for the right reason. She is attempting to take care of the body God gave her, rather than trying to get her mom's approval or fit into a size eight.

You may be thinking, "I can see how a negative body image could develop from being subjected to the kind of sexual trauma Marybeth went through, but why would I have cause to hate myself?" That's what I want you to think about in this next exercise—your own life experiences. I'll ask you to write down memories you have of yourself at different life stages. Perhaps you've never consciously thought about why you dislike the reflection in the mirror. It is important that you become conscious of exactly what is driving your dissatisfaction with your body in order to overcome it.

This may be a very difficult exercise for you. Most of us try to avoid these painful memories. You will have to trust me that stirring them up will be good for you in the end. As you write you may feel pain; you may even cry. On the other hand, if you have hardened yourself you may not feel anything. At this stage it is just important that you attempt to survey memories you have of your body during these life stages. We'll work on how to resolve your feelings (or get in touch with your feelings) in future chapters.

As you answer the following questions, try to picture yourself and how you looked at the time. If you have pictures of yourself at each stage, they will aid you in remembering how you felt. Leave some blank space in your journal after each stage of development. As you read this book, you may have more memories that you will want to record in the blank spaces.

I encourage you to pray and ask God to help you remember experiences you need to think about in order to receive healing from your pain. So let's get started on the exercise.

Body History Reflection: A Chronological Survey

As you read through the stages below, think back about how you felt about your body, and write down memories you have of those particular stages of development. Pay special attention to recalling specific statements people made about your body or their own bodies. For example, "My mom told me that after I was born, she gained 60 pounds." Or "My father told me he felt sorry for me because my skin was too dark."

Stage One: Preschool Years, Ages 0–6

How did your parents react to your body size? How did your parents care for your bodily and emotional needs? How did you discover that you were different from males? Did you undergo any major medical procedures?

Stage Two: School-Age Years, Grades 1–4

How did you relate to peers? Were you called names or teased? Did you have friends? How did you feel about your performance at school? Did you undergo any major medical procedures? How did you feel about the opposite sex? Was there any physical, sexual, mental, or emotional abuse? How did you feel about yourself in a bathing suit? How did your mother react to her body?

Stage Three: Puberty Years, Grades 5–8

How did you feel about the onset of menstruation? How did your friends talk about their own or your body? What did you think of your developing body? Did you know it's normal for girls to gain 20–40 pounds at this age? Did your parents and siblings accept your body? Did you undergo any major medical procedures that affected the way you felt toward your body? What did you like or dislike about your body?

Stage Four: High School Years, Grades 9–12

Were you the subject of teasing? How were you treated by the opposite sex? Did you think your body size or looks had an impact on dating?

Stage Five: Young Adult Years, Ages 18–29
Did you feel your appearance had an impact on your vocation, dating, or marriage? How did you think of your body on significant birthdays? How did you feel about yourself in a bathing suit? How did you feel about your body on your wedding day? How did you feel about your body during or after pregnancy? Were there any life events (divorce, job loss, and so on) that caused you to look down on your body?

Stage Six: Adult Years, Ages 30–55
Use some of the questions from above. How did you feel about your changing metabolism, gray hair, wrinkles?

Stage Seven: Senior Adult Years, 55+
Use some of the questions from above. Are there any major health issues that have affected how you see your body? How have you adjusted to changes related to aging?

    🌹 In doing the exercise above, did you discover any experiences that may have contributed to your poor image of yourself?

We will come back to these memories in later chapters. For now, it is good that you have been able to start considering why you feel the way you do about your body. Keep praying and asking God to reveal any hurt that you are harboring and need His healing for. As other memories come to mind, go back and write them down in this same section of your journal.

What Is a Healthy Body Image?

Of the three women talked about so far, Christine is the one with the healthiest body image. Yet, in the world's view she would be considered the least attractive because she is overweight. Why does she have a healthy body image? Read about what a healthy body image is, and you will better understand.

A healthy body image is characterized by three major components:

respect, care, and perspective. A woman with a healthy body image respects her body, takes care of her body, and keeps her body in perspective.

A Healthy Body Image Involves Respect
In Psalm 139:13–16 David is referring to his body.

> ¹³For you created my inmost being; you knit me together in my mother's womb. ¹⁴I praise you because I am fearfully and wonderfully made; your works are wonderful, I know that full well. ¹⁵My frame was not hidden from you when I was made in the secret place. When I was woven together in the depths of the earth, ¹⁶your eyes saw my unformed body. All the days ordained for me were written in your book before one of them came to be.

🌿 Why is David in awe of his body?

🌿 Have you ever pondered your body in the same way?

🌿 Write a psalm to God telling Him why you are in awe of the way you were made.

A healthy body image involves a sense of respect for the miracle your body is. Romans 1:20 says that the reality that there is a God who designed the universe is all around us every day. Even if your body has been handicapped, it is still a miraculous testimony of God our Creator.

When David proclaimed that his body was fearfully and wonderfully made, he was giving praise to God. Do you realize how many organs, blood vessels, muscles, and bones are involved when you just move your index finger up and down?

A person with a healthy body image respects the reality that God gave her a body as a gift. Others may not think the way you look is "all that." But God created you, and to Him you are "all that" and more! If you have a healthy body image, you will respect that you are fearfully and wonderfully made by a caring and loving God who has a plan for your life here on earth. If you feel ugly and made wrong, you have an unhealthy body image.

🌿 Check yourself:

_____ I know I have body flaws, but I recognize God made me the way I am.

_____ I still don't accept how I look.

A Healthy Body Image Involves Care

Satan knows that we look out for our bodies. In Job 2, after Satan had destroyed all the material possessions and children that Job loved, Satan approached God and the two had this conversation.

> [3]Then the Lord said to Satan, "Have you considered my servant Job? There is no one on earth like him; he is blameless and upright, a man who fears God and shuns evil. And he still maintains his integrity, though you incited me against him to ruin him without any reason." [4]"Skin for skin!" Satan replied. "A man will give all he has for his own life. [5]But stretch out your hand and strike his flesh and bones, and he will surely curse you to your face" (Job 2:3–5).

🌿 What was Satan's excuse for why Job had not given up on God?

🌿 Do you have a natural desire to protect your body from harm?

Satan knows that our natural, healthy instincts are to care for our bodies. When we are thinking of our bodies correctly, we won't allow harm to come to them. We will feed ourselves correctly, and we will get proper exercise and rest. We won't overwork ourselves.

Are you doing anything to your body to harm it? Do you care for your body correctly? If you are not taking care of your body, you do not have a healthy body image.

  ❦ Check yourself:

     _____ I eat right, and get some exercise and proper rest. I don't overwork my body.

     _____ There's room for improvement.

A Healthy Body Image Involves Perspective

In 2 Corinthians 10:12, Paul speaks of the futility of comparing ourselves to others.

> We do not dare to classify or compare ourselves with
> some who commend themselves. When they measure
> themselves by themselves and compare themselves with
> themselves, they are not wise.

  ❦ Is it also foolish to compare our physical attributes with others? Why or why not?

The world measures men and women by their looks, their talents, their money, and their power. God has a completely different measuring system. We aren't supposed to measure ourselves by other people. We should measure ourselves only by God's Word. The following passage from 1 Corinthians is referring to the work of the kingdom, but it could also apply to our physical attributes.

> [28]And in the church God has appointed first of all apostles, second prophets, third teachers, then workers of miracles, also those having gifts of healing, those able to help others, those with gifts of administration, and those

speaking in different kinds of tongues. [29]Are all apostles? Are all prophets? Are all teachers? Do all work miracles? [30]Do all have gifts of healing? Do all speak in tongues? Do all interpret? (1 Corinthians 12:28–30)

❧ How can your physical attributes affect the work God has given you to do in the kingdom?

❧ Do you think you need to have certain physical attributes or personality attributes to serve in the kingdom?

❧ If someone has "nicer" attributes than you, how are you supposed to feel about that person? About yourself?

God didn't create all of us to fit the latest concept of beautiful. We define beauty by our specific culture in a specific time. Marilyn Monroe, a beauty icon of the 1950s, would be considered fat in our culture today. Many beauties of today may not be considered beautiful in the future.

Look at how God created people. He created variety. He made different shades of skin color, a variety of eye color and hair. People are a rainbow of beauty in the eye of the Creator. It's our differences that make us beautiful. If you can't see the unique beauty in yourself and others, then you don't have a healthy body image.

❧ Check yourself:

_____ I can see beauty in myself and others. I don't define beauty by a runway model.

_____ I've got some work to do here.

This chapter lays the foundation for overcoming a negative body image. Next week you will do more work in confronting the false beliefs that trap you in body hate.

Discussion Questions

1. Have you ever felt the same way as the bride of Solomon in Song of Songs 1:6? Why do you think women obsess over their body flaws rather than enjoy the things that are right with their bodies?

2. What changed for the bride of Solomon so that she liked herself in Song of Songs 2:1? Did her skin color change?

3. Go around the room and share the most attractive physical characteristic (eyes, height, nose, hair, etc.) of the person on your right.

4. Go around the room and share the most positive character quality (kindness, generosity, thoughtfulness, etc.) of the person on your left.

5. Go around the room and state the physical characteristic you like best about yourself and thank God for it. (Thank you, God, that you gave me big brown eyes.)

6. How do you think God wants us to think about our bodies based on the information in Psalm 139:15–16—God knows our frame; God oversaw our creation; God knows how long we will live in these bodies while on earth; before we ever saw ourselves, He knew it all!

CHAPTER TWO

The Truth about Perfection

Imagine a world where everyone looked like Barbie and Ken dolls. Picture an entire group of people you know and interact with daily (males and females) looking this way. (Choose your work group, a class at school, a small group from church, your family, etc.) How do you think people would interact if every single person in that group looked like either Ken or Barbie? In your mind give the Ken and Barbie dolls the personalities of people you know. Imagine all the Kens dressed in the same outfit and all the Barbies dressed in the same outfit. Try to imagine yourself as a Barbie, talking to the other Barbies and Kens. Would you finally like yourself? Would you think you were as pretty as the other Barbies, whom you look exactly like? Would you be envious of the other Barbies? Would you think they were envious of you? Would everyone in the group be happy with how they looked? Would anyone be depressed? Would anyone struggle with body image? Would anyone feel better than everyone else based on how he or she looked?

Does this exercise conjure up images of a sci-fi movie to you? It's such an unreal and bizarre concept, you may find it hard to even think in this way. Try anyway. Think of how these people would interact if they all looked the same. It wouldn't take long for the individuals to find a way to look different from the rest of the group. The girls who needed to think of themselves as better than the others would do their hair in a different way to try to validate their importance. People would pierce and tattoo, cut and shave—anything to look unique and different from one another. If we all looked exactly the same, our inner imperfections would turn up in other ways. Perfection isn't achieved through having flat abs or firm breasts. In fact, you can never achieve perfection when it comes to your body. So why is beauty such a big illusion?

I wish I had bigger lips.

Some would blame Barbie herself for creating the illusion of perfection. Let's face it, Barbie is a total fantasy. Have you seen the statistics that demonstrate how impossible it would be for Barbie to exist in human form? "Exceptionally tall, but with a child's size three foot permanently molded in a high-heeled position, Barbie's measurements read 39-18-33."[1]

Now let's see how much perfectionism influences your thinking. Answer each question below true or false.

Perfection Scale

_____ Beautiful people have the best of life.

_____ I know that if people saw me before I get myself fixed up, they wouldn't like me at all.

_____ People will notice and think poorly of me if I have a blemish on my face.

_____ How people look reflects how valuable they are to society.

_____ If I eat cake (or other sweets) I will feel fat.

_____ The way I look is a big reason why I haven't achieved what I've wanted to in life.

_____ The only way I could ever be happy with the way I look is if I could change several of my physical characteristics.

_____ I believe that I can make my appearance what I want to if I spend a lot of money on the right kind of beauty products.

_____ If I can get my looks the right way, then I can have the relationships, job, joy, and peace that I want.

_____ I am ashamed of how I look.

Total number of true statements: _____

0	No perfectionism
1–2	Mild perfectionism
3–7	Moderate perfectionism
8–10	Severe perfectionism

Every one of these statements is perfectionist. They represent many of the wrong assumptions that affect our body images negatively. The more trues you have, the more you need to recognize the dangerous and suffocating problem of negative body image. Perhaps it's time to think about what fuels your perfectionism about your body.

The illusion and the quest for perfection has a history far deeper than Barbie dolls and modern culture. The problem of body image goes back to the time before the first man and woman were created. The true roots of a poor body image are found in the same source as misinformation and self-deception.

I still remember the first time each of my children lied to me. They were both around age five. Both of them looked me straight in the eye and told their first bold-faced lie. My husband and I always made a big deal about little lies. We did this because we wanted to raise our kids to think of lying as a serious offense. We also wanted to build a relationship with them that made them feel brave about telling us the truth, even though consequences would follow. One of the ways we emphasized the danger of lying is that we would ask them, "Who is the father of lies?" We would explain that Satan is the father of lies. We wanted them to associate lying with the very opposite of God. Neither wanted to follow in Satan's footsteps. I can't say that my children never lie to me. I think our parenting style has had an impact on them, and I do think they recognize that lying is a big deal and are more willing to tell the truth even if it hurts a little.

I want to say something similar to you about perfectionism. Satan is not called the father of perfectionism in the Bible, but he has a lot to teach us about what we need to avoid when it comes to beauty perfection. As you think about Satan's example when it comes to the perfectionism about how you look, I'm hoping it will prod you to avoid the traps of beauty perfection even more.

Let's look at Ezekiel 28, which is a controversial passage. Some scholars believe it refers to earthly kings, while others believe it is a prophetic passage referring to Satan. But for our purposes, let's consider what we can learn about Satan from this passage.

> [11]The word of the Lord came to me: [12] "Son of man, take up a lament concerning the king of Tyre and say to him: 'This is what the Sovereign Lord says: You were the model of perfection, full of wisdom and perfect in beauty. [13]You were in Eden, the garden of God; every precious stone adorned you: ruby, topaz and emerald, chrysolite, onyx and jasper, sapphire, turquoise, and beryl. Your settings and mountings were made of gold; on the day you were created they were prepared. [14]You were anointed as a guardian cherub, for so I ordained you. You were on the holy mount of God; you walked among the fiery stones. [15]You were blameless in your ways from the day you were created till wickedness was found in you. [16]Through your widespread

trade you were filled with violence, and you sinned. So I
drove you in disgrace from the mount of God, and I expelled
you, O guardian cherub, from among the fiery stones. [17]Your
heart became proud on account of your beauty, and you corrupted your wisdom because of your splendor. So I threw
you to the earth; I made a spectacle of you before kings. [18]By
your many sins and dishonest trade you have desecrated your
sanctuaries. So I made a fire come out from you, and it consumed you, and I reduced you to ashes on the ground in the
sight of all who were watching. [19]All the nations who knew
you are appalled at you; you have come to a horrible end and
will be no more' " (Ezekiel 28:11–19).

❧ What did Satan look like when God created him?

God created Satan in awesome beauty and splendor. He was the
model of perfection—the measuring stick for what is beautiful in
God's creation. Nowhere in the rest of creation could there be found
a being that could compare to the beauty he possessed. It's hard for us
to imagine the description as something we would judge as beautiful,
however. We would be more likely to accept the Barbie doll as a measuring stick of beauty than a being called a cherub adorned with precious stones in settings of gold. Somehow these words don't evoke the
awesome reality of how beautiful and perfect God created Satan to be.
We just have to trust that if a heavenly beauty pageant had been held,
Satan would have won hands down. Everyone could recognize a perfect beauty in him that outshone others.

God didn't just make Satan beautiful, though; He also made him
wise. It would have been unfair of God to give him that kind of beauty
without the wisdom to go along with it. Without wisdom he may
have had an excuse for desiring to exalt himself above God. But
although Satan did possess wisdom, he didn't use it to glorify God.

❧ Why did Satan turn away from God? (See Ezekiel 28:17 above.)

It was Satan's beauty that first turned his heart to wickedness. It made his heart proud, and that pride corrupted his wisdom. Where once his beauty glorified the Creator who had granted such wonder, now his beauty made him think he could glorify himself even more through his own effort. His corrupt wisdom told him that he could become more by taking over God's kingdom.

❧ What will happen to Satan in the end? (See vv. 18–19)

This passage is one of the many prophesies about Satan's desperate destiny. Where once he walked on the fiery stones, there will come a day when he will be consumed by fire. Many will be looking at him then, but they won't be admiring his beauty. They will be appalled at him instead.

Now let's look at Genesis 3:14–15:

> ¹⁴So the Lord God said to the serpent, "Because you have done this, cursed are you above all the livestock and all the wild animals! You will crawl on your belly and you will eat dust all the days of your life. ¹⁵And I will put enmity between you and the woman, and between your offspring and hers; he will crush your head, and you will strike his heel."

❧ What did the serpent look like when God cursed him?

Evidently, after Satan was cast down to earth when he sinned, he still desired to use wisdom and beauty for influence. When he came in the form of an animal to tempt the man and woman, he chose the serpent. The serpent was the craftiest of all the wild animals. When God judged the serpent, He made the serpent the lowliest and most dreaded of all the livestock and wild animals. God made the serpent crawl on his belly and eat dust all his existence on earth. This is a picture of what had already happened to Satan. Although he can disguise himself as an angel of light (2 Corinthians 11:14), he has lost all the beauty that once adorned his very being. It's also a picture of God's plan to send Jesus Christ. The seed of woman (Christ) would crush his head, and the serpent would strike His heel. On the cross Jesus' heel was struck, but at the resurrection Satan's head was crushed!

Let's look at another controversial passage that can be applied to Satan, Isaiah 14:11–15:

> ¹¹All your pomp has been brought down to the grave,
> along with the noise of your harps; maggots are spread
> out beneath you and worms cover you. ¹²How you have
> fallen from heaven, O morning star, son of the dawn! You
> have been cast down to the earth, you who once laid low
> the nations! ¹³You said in your heart, "I will ascend to
> heaven; I will raise my throne above the stars of God; I
> will sit enthroned on the mount of assembly, on the
> utmost heights of the sacred mountain. ¹⁴I will ascend
> above the tops of the clouds; I will make myself like the
> Most High." ¹⁵But you are brought down to the grave, to
> the depths of the pit.

❧ How do these verses describe Satan? (vv. 11–12)

Satan has lost all of his pomp in his present condition. He was once a bright and morning star in heaven, but he will eventually be cast down to the grave with maggots and worms. Satan isn't there yet, but there is a day and time when God will make good on his promises to Satan.

❧ What were the five "I will" statements that Satan made?

Let's look at the five "I will" statements and compare them to the truth.

Satan said:	**The Truth:**
1. I will ascend to heaven.	I will recognize God's loving, ruling power in my life.
2. I will raise my throne above the stars of God.	I will keep God on the throne and bow down from mine.
3. I will sit enthroned on the mount of the assembly.	I will worship with the others in the assembly.
4. I will ascend above the tops of the clouds.	I will let God lift me up in His time.
5. I will make myself like the Most High.	I will serve God faithfully.

🌿 How do you think having a poor body image compares with trying to make yourself like God?

I believe poor body image has its roots far deeper than advertising and cultural influences (although I do agree, those influences are powerful). I believe that poor body image has close connections to original sin, by way of the originator of sin, Satan himself. *The spiritual root of all body image struggles is doubting God's goodness in the way He made you.* I don't know anyone who struggles with a poor body image who would say that she is trying to be beautiful so she can worship God fully. I do know that every human sinner desires to be accepted, to be better than others, and to stand out. This is at the root of all body loathing that fills the earth.

Prayer is a powerful tool in overcoming the trap of negative body image. There is nothing Satan would enjoy more than getting women to feel ugly and useless in God's kingdom. Let's learn from Satan's wicked example and move away from being consumed by beauty and perfectionism.

Open Your Eyes to Authentic Perfection

Jesus came to earth to bring us to perfection. There is only one way to this perfection, and that is through Him. The perfection He brings is not the same kind we are seeking in our physical bodies. The essence of perfection is sinlessness, which we will ultimately experience in heaven.

My husband is attracted to thin women who appear to have breast implants, yet he says he would never want me to do that to my body. It's hard for me to believe that I am attractive to him.

We will be given new bodies when we get to heaven. I can guarantee they won't be as silly and unimaginative as the American cultural ideals Barbie and Ken. We aren't told a lot about these bodies. We know that they will not be limited by the same kind of sexual relationships as on earth. Matthew 22:30 says, "At the resurrection people will neither marry nor be given in marriage; they will be like the angels in heaven." Our bodies will not be limited by the same physical boundaries. Jesus walked through closed doors and ascended into heaven (John 20:19, 26; Luke 24:51). Interestingly, our bodies will still consume food to some degree. After His resurrection, Jesus ate the fish the disciples gave Him (Luke 24:42–43). Jesus will eat and drink with us again in heaven (Luke 22:16).

Just as you'll never have the perfect body without God, you can't have a perfect heart without God. You are growing to understand the perfection that Jesus wants to bring as you are freed from a negative body image. When you are feeling defeated, made wrong, and ugly, it holds you back spiritually. That is why it is important to see how your negative body image developed, so you can allow God to reveal the beauty He created in you. If you don't realize God's beauty in you, you will remain at your level of self-loathing, keep trying endless ways to fix your body flaws, or continue to build up new reasons to hate your body. This may lead to a deeper trap of depression, anxiety, eating disorders, and the like.

How Does Body Image Develop?

Body image is what you think you look like on the outside. Body image changes from day to day. For example, Karen is the prettiest woman in her circle of friends. When she is out to lunch with them and around town, she never struggles with her body image. She thinks she looks good and goes on with her life with little concern about how she looks. But when someone enters her world who is prettier than she is, she's flooded with insecurity. Suddenly the 10 pounds she has gained becomes an inner tube around her stomach, and she feels like the ugliest woman in the world.

Even though a part of me knows I am attractive and I get whistled at on the street, deep inside I still feel like the fat 10 year old that no one thought was anything special.

Physical comparisons go through your mind every day. You aren't always aware of them and how they affect you. Subtle toxins have damaged your sense of self. In the first chapter, you took a chronological overview of how you felt about your body. The following exercises will help you identify what blocks you from seeing your true beauty.

Name Exercise

1. In your journal, write down any names that others called you from your childhood to the present. Write names you can remember, whether positive or negative, names that described your body, or other characteristics attributed to you.

2. If this name exercise brings up memories you haven't written in your chronological survey, go back and record them there.

3. Out of obedience to Christ and your desire to fully receive God's healing, go back over your list and mark out any negative names you were called.

4. Write 1 John 3:1 across the bottom of your page: "How great is the love the Father has lavished on us, that we should be called children of God! And that is what we are!" Underneath the scripture write out the statement, "I will be called _____ (your first name), God's daughter. From now on, I will not answer to any other name."

Five Senses Overview

You developed your opinions about your body through various senses and experiences over the years. There are five main senses and experiences through which you gather the data that sums up your body image. Your body image consists of:

- visual information (what you see);
- mental information (what you think about what you see);
- emotional information (feelings you associate with how you look);
- kinetic information (how your body functions and moves); and
- historical information (what you remember about how others have reacted to your body).

All of this information has combined over time to make up your body image. Most of the time you are not consciously aware of these senses recording information, but they do.

Answering the following questions will help you evaluate what your body image is right now.

Current Inventory of Your Body Image

1. Visual. In your journal list your top five positive and negative physical characteristics.

2. Mental. On a scale of 1–10, 1 being "I think I should wear a bag over my entire body," and 10 being "I am very satisfied with how I look," write down how you evaluate your looks right now.

3. Emotional. In your journal write down the following sentence and the feeling or feelings that best describe you: "When I look at myself in the mirror, I feel . . ." (Here are a few examples to get you started: depressed, embarrassed, confident, proud, ashamed, rejected, happy, joyful, content.)

4. Kinetic. Name at least one activity you enjoy participating in with your body. "I appreciate that with my body I can . . ." (For example, play soccer, dance, ride a bike, feel the breeze, climb hills, hug someone.)

5. Historical. What statement below is most true of your experiences? Record that statement in your journal.

_____ I remember very few times when I felt a great deal of shame about my body either because of what others said about me, or because I wanted to do something (a cartwheel, shoot a basket, and so on) that I couldn't do.

_____ I can recall at least five significant times that I was shamed about my body by others' comments or actions toward me.

_____ I have had considerably more negative comments about or actions toward my body than positive comments or actions.

It's critical for you to acknowledge how often your negative body image has been reinforced over your lifetime. When a statement is reinforced over and over, it takes on a sense of truth, even if it is not true. Negative feelings, experiences, and comments combine into a powerful force that blinds you from seeing who you really are.

You Can Overcome a Negative Body Image

Do you identify any consistencies between your chronological survey in chapter one and the way you answered the questions listed here? For instance, Susan, the 16-year-old bulimic, said her most positive feature was her brown eyes, and negative, her big bottom. When she compared that to what she wrote in her chronological survey in chapter one, she remembered how her dad used to sing to her about her big brown eyes, and how most of the guys in the cafeteria put girls down the most about their behinds. For Susan there was a direct correlation.

As you look back over your responses, the impact of your experiences on your body image will become more obvious to you. The more negative your experiences with your body have been, the more self- and body-rejecting you are. But you do not have to be imprisoned by these experiences. In fact, just bringing them into your conscious awareness gives you more power over them and their negative influence on how you see yourself.

I don't have eyebrows or eyelashes that you can see.
I use makeup to look better, but I wish I could be normal.

Personally, I didn't think much about my body until I was about 12 or 13. Before then, I was frustrated that I couldn't do a cartwheel, but proud that I could swim three lengths of my pool in one breath. Suddenly, something happened. I grew taller. I had always been painfully thin. But when I was 13, thin was in. I began getting attention from older guys at my school. Many people commented that I could be a model.

But then there were the *other* comments. I didn't develop in the breast area. This became open opportunity for painful comments. In spite of that, I discovered a new avenue to gaining approval as a female. I found that if I looked good—if I enhanced my appearance with makeup and clothes—I could ward off unwanted rejection and receive approval.

Then in the midst of my early adolescence, when I wasn't even seeking God, He showed me a secret that kept me a little more sane and less depressed than many of the girls I meet these days. It is the secret to true beauty.

I distinctly remember being 14 years old and looking in a magazine while dreaming of modeling someday. As I turned the pages of that magazine the reality of how many beautiful people there are in the world overwhelmed me. I thought to myself, *I could never be the prettiest; I'd better develop some other qualities.* At that time I wasn't listening to God's voice in my life. I was a Christian, but out of touch with God. Now I know it was God who was showing me where true beauty can be found. We are fooling ourselves if we believe having the perfect looks will make us happy inside. Some of the world's most beautiful people are the ones most torn by heartache, broken relationships, and even poor body image. The secret to true beauty is being at peace with who you are.

God gave me another perspective on how He might have protected me because of my body flaws. I must admit, I'm thankful for my small breasts. Thinking of all the attention I began to receive between the ages of 13 and 15 and knowing how far I was from yielding to God's direction for my life, I realize that feeling negatively about my body actually helped me not get in trouble sexually. If I had felt more confident about how sexy I was, I might have compromised even more in my rebellion during those years.

I must admit too, that as a mother of a teen myself, I still feel the pressure to look good. It's not as extreme as it is for those who are 12 to 21, but it's there. I have thoughts that my stomach is too round, my breasts too small. However, I refuse to worry about my arms wagging in the wind! When I find myself succumbing, I remember the secret to overcoming a negative body image is letting God show me my true beauty. Believe me, it's great to know the pressure to look good doesn't have to rule my life. Celebrating rather than debasing my body is a wonderful way to live.

How Do We Stop the Perfection Cycle?

In later chapters, you will work on exercises that will help you stop the raging war of perfectionist assumptions. But for now, commit your heart through prayer to finding and doing what God says is best. Pray this prayer from your heart:

> Dear heavenly Father and creator of my body:
> I recognize that I struggle to know and live out what is truly perfect. I can see how my heart is drawn to Satan's

message that perfectionism is the answer. I can easily get focused on wanting perfect beauty rather than wanting You. In the strong name of Jesus Christ I stand against the world of advertising, diet, the beauty industry, my vanity, and Satan himself. I resist every force that would seek to distract me from who I really am and what You desire for me to do in, and through, this body You gave me. I reject the distorted concepts and ideas that make body perfection sound plausible and desirable. I oppose every attempt to keep me from knowing full fellowship with You. I commit to completing this study with an open heart to be transformed into true perfection through Jesus Christ. Amen.

Discussion Questions

1. What do you consider perfect beauty?

2. Why do you think God created us with so many different variations in appearance?

3. Go over each of the 10 statements on the Perfection Scale on pages 28–29 and discuss why they are perfectionist and not true assumptions.

4. Why could Satan be called "the father of beauty perfectionism"?

5. At what times or in what situations do you struggle with your body image the most?

6. Share prayer requests about how you are finding victory or defeat over body image, as well as other issues for which you need prayer. Repeat the prayer on pages 40–41 in unison as you close your meeting.

CHAPTER THREE

Why Our Bodies Were Created

Have you ever built a house? We bought our house when it was almost finished, so the majority of decisions were already made. By the time I finished picking out knobs and pulls for the kitchen and baths, door handles, light fixtures, carpet, and tile, I was grateful that the earlier decisions had already been made. When God created our bodies, the sky was the limit. He could have made us without the need for sleep, or to be perfectly nourished by one meal a month. But He didn't. He made us just the way we are.

My son, Benjamin, often asks me to explain some of God's decisions. He's great with the "why" questions. He will wonder, "Why did God make girls grow faster than boys?" I can't always give Benjamin an exact answer to his questions, but I can be sure that God has a reason. In fact, God isn't ashamed of the bodies He created for us. God doesn't judge us by what our bodies look like either.

Nowhere in God's Word is anyone put down for his or her body.

You never find God putting one of His prophets on a diet, unless it was a spiritual discipline such as fasting, abstaining from certain foods, and so on. God doesn't hold beauty contests or make comparisons. To God, every body is beautiful. No exceptions!

Genesis 1: The Creation of Bodies

Genesis gives us a unique look at the importance of our bodies. There is a lot in this book that helps us understand ourselves and the differences between men and women. I've written all about that in a different book (*A Woman's Search for Worth*, Focus on the Family/ Tyndale, 2002). Genesis 1–2 also gives us volumes of great information about how our bodies were created and God's purpose for them. Let's look at Genesis 1:26–27.

> [26]Then God said, "Let us make man in our image, in our likeness, and let them rule over the fish of the sea and the birds of the air, over the livestock, over all the earth, and over all the creatures that move along the ground." [27]So God created man in his own image, in the image of God he created him; male and female he created them.

🌿 God created man and woman in His own image. How is that reflected in our bodies?

God does not exist in human form. He is spirit. Being created in the image of God means we reflect His spirit inside us. There are several passages in Scripture in which certain prophets and leaders saw visions of God and Jesus with bodily qualities.

Match the following passages with the visual manifestations of God's or Jesus' body in the scriptures beneath.

_____ Moses saw God's back after He removed His hand.

_____ Isaiah saw God seated on a throne with a train that filled the temple.

_____ Daniel saw one who looked like the son of man dressed in linen, with a body, face, eyes, arms, and legs that gleamed in different ways.

_____ John saw Jesus with hair like wool, white as snow, with eyes, feet, and face that glowed.

Revelation 1:12–17:

[12]I turned around to see the voice that was speaking to me. And when I turned I saw seven golden lampstands, [13]and among the lampstands was someone "like a son of man," dressed in a robe reaching down to his feet and with a golden sash around his chest. [14]His head and hair were white like wool, as white as snow, and his eyes were like blazing fire. [15]His feet were like bronze glowing in a furnace, and his voice was like the sound of rushing waters. [16]In his right hand he held seven stars, and out of his mouth came a sharp double-edged sword. His face was like the sun shining in all its brilliance. [17]When I saw him, I fell at his feet as though dead. Then he placed his right hand on me and said: "Do not be afraid. I am the First and the Last."

Daniel 10:5–6:

[5]I looked up and there before me was a man dressed in linen, with a belt of the finest gold around his waist. [6]His body was like chrysolite, his face like lightning, his eyes like flaming torches, his arms and legs like the gleam of burnished bronze, and his voice like the sound of a multitude.

Exodus 33:17–23:

[17]And the Lord said to Moses, "I will do the very thing you have asked, because I am pleased with you and I know you by name." [18]Then Moses said, "Now show me your glory." [19]And the Lord said, "I will cause all my

goodness to pass in front of you, and I will proclaim my
name, the Lord, in your presence. I will have mercy on
whom I will have mercy, and I will have compassion on
whom I will have compassion. [20]But," he said, "you cannot see my face, for no one may see me and live." [21]Then
the Lord said, "There is a place near me where you may
stand on a rock. [22]When my glory passes by, I will put
you in a cleft in the rock and cover you with my hand
until I have passed by. [23]Then I will remove my hand and
you will see my back; but my face must not be seen."

Isaiah 6:1–4:

[1]In the year that King Uzziah died, I saw the Lord seated
on a throne, high and exalted, and the train of his robe
filled the temple. [2]Above him were seraphs, each with six
wings: With two wings they covered their faces, with two
they covered their feet, and with two they were flying.
[3]And they were calling to one another: "Holy, holy, holy is
the Lord Almighty; the whole earth is full of his glory."
[4]At the sound of their voices the doorposts and thresholds
shook and the temple was filled with smoke.

Do you like your back, face, hands, arms, legs, and hair? Would you
like to be seated on a throne or be dressed in linen and gold? These are
some of the physical manifestations of Jesus and God. When I stop and
think about it from God's perspective, not liking my hair is an insult to
my Creator. Jesus' hair in Revelation is described as looking like white
wool. That might not be considered attractive to a New York hairdresser! He or she probably wouldn't be too impressed with my hair
either. Does it really matter? I'm just glad that Jesus is coming back for
me, white-wool hair and all. I don't care what His hair looks like.

God sees me the same way. He isn't impressed when I have a good
hair day. Rather, He is impressed when I love my husband out of obedience to Him. He only cares about my hair in caring about me.

Matthew 10:30 tells us that He knows the number of hairs on my head. If I ask Him to help me get my hair to look right for a particular speaking engagement or event, He often does and I feel His care. But God never cares about whether my hair looks like the latest fad. He does care that I love and obey Him. When you are thinking about your relationship with God, does your dissatisfaction with your body become less significant?

Genesis 2: The Creation of Our Bodies

The Lord God formed the man from the dust of the
ground and breathed into his nostrils the breath of life,
and the man became a living being (Genesis 2:7).

Try to imagine this scene in your mind. Picture God picking up some of the dust He had created on the third day. Watch Him forming the dirt into the shape of a human male body. See the body lifeless, existing in the form of a man, but without movement or other signs of life. Then observe as the God who made the figure moves toward him and presses close enough to breathe into his nostrils. Watch as that figure, receiving the breath of life, becomes a living being. Can you imagine anything more meaningful and miraculous?

The experience that comes closest to this in our journey on earth is the birth of children. A healthy birth is one of the most joyful events our existence here on earth has to offer. The births of my two children were two of the most sacred moments of my life. If you have ever birthed a child or been present at a birth, remember that occasion as you answer the following questions.

How do you think God feels about the man He has made?

What do you think is the most amazing aspect of the human body? (For example, the nervous system, the body's ability to fight off disease, the fact that it breathes in and out, how soft the skin is.)

Everything God made was good. He didn't want to melt Adam down and start over. He was very pleased with the final touch of His creation we call the universe.

Imagine that God has just created you in the garden. Look at your body right now. Don't look in a mirror, just look at the parts of your body that you can see with your own eyes.

> ❧ Find 10 parts of your body that you can praise God for. Give Him praise as the Master Creator of your body. Look at your toes and watch them wiggle. Praise God for making our toes to wiggle. Rub your hands together and feel the smoothness and warmth. Thank God that you can feel comfort through a touch.

> ❧ Thinking back to God as the creator of our bodies, how do you think God feels when we hate and abuse the flesh that He made? How would you feel if you were the creator?

Marybeth noticed her fingernails first when she looked down at her body in the previous exercise. They were sculpted in a French manicure, a must for Marybeth. She would head straight to the nail salon if one of her nails broke, sure that everyone would notice. Now she just sat and stared at them. They were perfect. They were strong from the acrylic that was painted on them each week.

I'm embarrassed by the places I have hair.

Marybeth noticed something underneath her fingernails to thank God for. She recognized that fingernails weren't created to be one more area to worry about looking beautiful. She thought about their function. She praised God for creating fingernails to protect the sensitive skin underneath them. She thought to herself, *Even if my fingernails weren't perfectly manicured, they would do their job.* Then a deeper thought struck her. *I don't have to turn my fingernails into a display of my worthiness. My fingernails can do the job they were created to do without beauty treatment.*

It wasn't a life-changing exercise by any means, but it did make her think about her body a little bit differently. It actually stirred up the thought that maybe there were parts of her body that she really could be proud of. Perhaps she did indeed have value in this life.

How to Really Love Your Body

Bruce Springsteen wrote, "It's a sad man, my friend, who is living in his own skin, but can't stand the company."[1] His lyric wasn't about negative body image; it was about self-loathing in general. Body hate is a specific form of self-loathing. Bruce Springsteen was right; it is a sad reality.

Self-loathing comes naturally to you. It is a part of your sin nature. Self-acceptance is supernatural; it requires God's grace. When you begin to get God's perspective of your body and turn down the other messages that drive you to dislike your body, you will find yourself loving your body for the right reasons. The source of all the self-loathing of your body that you participate in is based on your own fear of being rejected by others as much as you reject yourself. Rejecting yourself takes up a great deal of time and energy. I would like you to take inventory of how much energy you spend hating yourself.

Finding the Energy to Heal

1. How much time do you spend each day working on your body—applying makeup, exercising, fixing your hair, dressing, and so on?
2. How much time do you spend each month? Multiply your daily time, and add nail appointments, shopping for clothes and beauty products, hairdresser appointments, and so on.
3. How much time do you spend per day thinking about, examining, and fantasizing about fixing your body flaws?

Exercising three times a week helps increase my totals to 30 hours a month. If your exercise isn't excessive, then that is a good reason to spend time on your body; it does take time to exercise properly. If your beauty routines require more than 40 hours per month, there probably is room for you to think about why you commit so much time to beauty. Are you in bondage to fear of rejection?

Carol couldn't stand the size of her arms. She thought they revealed to the world a secret she could keep with the right clothes: that she really was a fat nobody. She had spent days shopping for a prom dress with sleeves or a wrap that could disguise her disgrace. She found nothing. Carol just rolled her eyes when I challenged her to wear the sleeveless dress she liked to her prom. To her, I was an out-of-touch middle-aged woman who didn't understand what is really important in the life of a 17 year old. No one could convince her that her arms looked fine. There was no way she would be free to have fun at her prom. She was consumed with frustration, hatred, and bad feelings. Her negative thoughts consumed her and drained her of the energy to enjoy living.

I have more freckles than anyone I know.

Carol's totals ended up being 60 hours per month, plus the time she spent incessantly thinking about her body flaws. Something had to give. She longed to find a dress that she could feel good about when she went to her prom. She wanted peace, but she was caught in a trap of self-loathing.

Carol and I discussed the emotional trap that had clamped down on her arms. We compared it to the kind of traps hunters use to catch wild animals. The more she struggled with her hate of her arms, the deeper the trap pressed into her skin and held her back. I asked, "How do you get out of a trap like that?" Carol realized that the solution was to stop focusing on her arms. If she were caught in a trap, she would look for a way to open the hinge. The hinge to the trap of body hate was to learn how to love her body in a healthy way. Carol didn't need to spend more time trying to make her body better. She needed to make time to accept the body God blessed her with.

I was always the brunt of schoolboy comments. They tore me apart from my hair to my big rear. I'm 45, but I still carry their brutal pronouncements with me every day.

Carol chose two of the suggested exercises below to help her fight her natural tendency to hate herself. Even though she didn't believe they would help much, she did them because at least they would interrupt the amount of time and energy she spent berating herself. She was kind to herself by taking a bubble bath and by taking her dog for a half-hour walk while thanking God for her body. These exercises weren't an instant fix, but they did stop her hopelessness for a period of time. They diverted her from her arm obsession.

Choose one or more of the following exercises to do this week.

1. Sit on a bench at a mall and find positive physical features on everyone who walks by.
2. Start a list of things you can do with your body. Try to build it to 100.
3. Type or print Psalm 139:14 on a sticky note or index card and put it on your mirror. Read it over before you leave your house.
4. Remember a time when you weren't consumed with disliking your body. Think about how you felt then and purpose to have those same feelings now.
5. Do a physical activity that is gentle to your body. Don't do it to lose weight, but to feel good and be stronger.

6. Make arrangements to sleep in as late as you can one day. When you awake, thank God for the rest your body received, then stretch out and enjoy the pleasure of that rest.

7. Get a massage.

8. As you lie down at night, thank God for all the activities you could do or participate in because you have a body.

9. Wrestle with a child or play with your dog. Get down on the floor and enjoy a good playtime.

10. Take a walk with God and thank Him for your body as you walk.

As you begin practicing these exercises regularly, you will find a new energy to heal. The energy comes from the time you are able to put into thinking positively about your body and interrupting the ways you are stuck in putting down your body. Body hate breeds more body hate.

God Loves You Just the Way You Are

Not liking your body is a symptom of not knowing who you are to God. First John 4:18 says, "There is no fear in love." Your fear of being unacceptable is evidence that you are not fully embracing God's acceptance of you. Being immersed in God's love is the remedy for discouragement about how you look. When you become energized by His love and acceptance, you'll find balance in your efforts to care for your body. You'll no longer eat and exercise better out of fear and shame.

> ✿ Write a letter to yourself from God expressing His love for you and how He wants you to think about your body.

If God did write you a letter expressing His love for you and how He wants you to feel about your body, this is what I think He might say.

> Dear _____ (your name):
> I want you to know the joy of believing you are wonderfully made (Psalm 139:14). Indeed, you are made just right! Satan is trying to deceive you into thinking your

_____ (body flaw) is evidence that I don't love you, but that is another one of his lies. I love you completely! I know everything about you and nothing stops me from loving you (Romans 8:38–39). I understand that you wish you didn't have _____ (body flaw). But you will miss out on what is important on earth if you don't receive your limitations and body flaws as part of my plan for you (Psalm 139:15–17). Bring all your worries to me, and I will replace them with peace (Matthew 11:28–30). I have great and wonderful opportunities for you to share my love with others in your world who don't know how much I love them, too. Receive my truth that you are beautiful, and let me show you the beautiful life I want you to have (1 Peter 3:5–6).

What else would God say? What has He been saying to you through this study? Get started on your letter and share it with a friend.

Discussion Questions

1. Why did God create our bodies?

2. How can we use our bodies to honor God?

3. How does your body reflect God's image?

4. What are some of the bodily characteristics that God revealed about Himself? Did thinking about them make you see those characteristics in yourself any differently?

5. Share with the group any shortcuts that you have discovered to help you care for your body while saving time, money, and effort.

6. Share with the group your experiences of doing the exercises this week.

CHAPTER FOUR

God's Word: The Body Manufacturer's Instructions

❧

As a small child, Katy was diagnosed with severe learning difficulties. Beginning in first grade she was sent to the "discovery room" for help with reading. Eventually she ended up in a remedial classroom with those she considered the "other stupid kids." It didn't matter what label the teachers gave her, the label she gave herself was "idiot." She felt utterly stupid all her life. Yet one aspect of herself that she regarded as special was her appearance. She always kept her nails polished and worked on her makeup and hair with extra pride. It was a cover for the sick and self-deprecating feelings she harbored inside.

It wasn't until her senior year that her pride in her looks took over her life. Her attempt to compensate with attractiveness led to anorexia. Eventually, she stopped being pretty at all. What Katy needed all along was an understanding of God, His love, and His instructions for caring for her body. The truths of God's Word would have directed her not to put too much emphasis on her looks as a remedy for low self-esteem. It's sad that Katy didn't learn these truths before she endured the hidden horrors of anorexia.

Hating your body is a sign that something is out of balance in your life. When an infant suffers from Failure to Thrive Syndrome, it is necessary for doctors and parents to figure out what is missing from the baby's environment that it needs in order to live. When you have a "failure to thrive" because your disapproval of your body holds you back from living and enjoying life, you need to figure out what is missing from your life.

My most humiliating experience of being overweight was the day I got kicked off the amusement park ride because I couldn't buckle the seatbelt. I left my family to enjoy the ride and walked the plank into deeper shame and contempt for who I am.

God has given you clear instructions for caring for the body He gave you. Read His manufacturer's instructions (the Bible) and look for ways you may be ignoring what your body needs, thus contributing to your "failure to thrive." Where are you missing understanding and obedience to God's Word and His purpose for your body? What truths from His Word can we explore here to lead to a healthy appreciation for body care?

The Manufacturer's Instructions for Body Care

We've already seen that God—your Manufacturer—created your body in His image. Rest assured that the Bible—God's instruction manual—provides you with very specific instructions about how to care for your body.

❧ As you read the following Scripture passages, comment in your journal about how you can best take care of your body.

1. Don't worry about your bodily needs; God will provide for you.

[25]Therefore I tell you, do not worry about your life, what you will eat or drink; or about your body, what you will wear. Is not life more important than food, and the body more important than clothes? [26]Look at the birds of the air; they do not sow or reap or store away in barns, and yet your heavenly Father feeds them. Are you not much more valuable than they? [27]Who of you by worrying can add a single hour to his life? [28]And why do you worry about clothes? See how the lilies of the field grow. They do not labor or spin. [29]Yet I tell you that not even Solomon in all his splendor was dressed like one of these. [30]If that is how God clothes the grass of the field, which is here today and tomorrow is thrown into the fire, will he not much more clothe you, O you of little faith? [31]So do not worry, saying, "What shall we eat?" or "What shall we drink?" or "What shall we wear?" [32]For the pagans run after all these things, and your heavenly Father knows that you need them. [33]But seek first his kingdom and his righteousness, and all these things will be given to you as well (Matthew 6:25–33).

❧ Has God ever provided clothes for you?

❧ Has God ever given you food?

❧ Why do you think God wants us to seek Him as a way to provide for our bodies?

Your life is more than what you put on, put in, or experience with, your body. It is natural for people to worry about issues that concern their bodies. God is trying to tell us that if we learn to trust Him with our natural bodily concerns, He will provide for them. God knows what our bodies need. He wants us to trust Him to provide for our nakedness, our hunger, and even the number of days we will live on this earth.

We rarely give God credit for meeting our daily needs. Have you thanked God for the food you've eaten today? Have you recognized God's provision in the clothes on your back right now?

I had open-heart surgery and my chest and stomach look like a tic-tac-toe board from the unsightly scars.

In my own life I recognize that God has provided clothes for me, and even certain dresses in answer to specific prayers. I remember a Christmas season when times were extra tight financially. I was to attend a Christmas party but didn't like the clothes I had to wear. While I was out Christmas shopping, I prayed that God would help me find a dress for the party for under $30. I found a dress I liked on the sale rack for $29.99. I was so grateful for it as I went up to the counter to pay. When the sales clerk rang it up at the register, the total came to $11.99. There was some kind of extra discount on sale items that day. God showed me that indeed He does do more than I could ever ask or think (Ephesians 3:20).

The amount of time we spend worrying about what we will wear reveals the level of our trust in God. When we seek God first, we discover how "all these things" are taken care of by God. We either learn that we don't need certain items after all, or we see God blessing us far beyond our understanding.

2. Don't worry about your body as much as about your soul.

> [28]Do not be afraid of those who kill the body but cannot
> kill the soul. Rather, be afraid of the One who can

destroy both soul and body in hell. [29]Are not two sparrows sold for a penny? Yet not one of them will fall to the
ground apart from the will of your Father. [30]And even the
very hairs of your head are all numbered. [31]So don't be
afraid; you are worth more than many sparrows
(Matthew 10:28–31).

🌿 Who or what murders your soul?

🌿 Why should you be as afraid of that as you are of murderers?

It is natural to fear those who can kill our bodies. We are afraid of
attack dogs, rapists, murderers, and drunk drivers. Each of these can
kill us or inflict great harm on our bodies. Our natural response is fear.
But do we fear the murder that may be taking place in our souls? Do
we assess the damage that body hate does to who we are and how we
see ourselves? God encourages us to have the same kind of fear of soul
murderers as we do of body murderers. My soul has been damaged by
materialism, anger, bitterness, business, covetousness, and more. The
frightening reality about soul murder is that it is a silent killer. Many
times the victim doesn't even recognize that her soul is dead.

I still remember the day I noticed a deadness in my soul. I was a
young mom and my husband was at the top of his field at a very
young age. All I thought about was the house I could buy, the car I
could drive, and the clothes I could wear. I was a regular attender of
church, but an infrequent worshiper of God. My soul was dead. Then
God gave me the job of chairing an AIDS committee, a potentially
divisive and disruptive issue in a church in the 1980s.

Even though my soul was dead, I recognized that the most important thing our committee needed to do was pray. We were fervent in
prayer for our church members as they responded to the information
that we brought before them. We prayed for wisdom as we prepared
our church nurseries and children's areas for the children and adults
inflicted with that terrible disease which brought so much pain, hurt,

and misunderstanding. God blessed in every way, and His will was accomplished in that church. That in itself was wonderful.

During that experience my soul came back to life. My soul was revived by the faith required to successfully lead that committee and our church to a compassionate and wise response to individuals inflicted with AIDS. I hadn't realized that my soul was dead, and evidently others hadn't either, or I would never have been asked to chair that committee.

Waking up from spiritual deadness is a powerful experience. When you aren't aware that you are spiritually dead, you don't feel a thing. You go about your life in the same way you always have. When you come in out of the cold and start feeling the warmth of God's presence again, it begins to hurt a little. I was humbled and scared; I knew I was in way over my head. I was embarrassed that my faith had shriveled and was so far from where it had been when I was a teenager. It hurt to face the truth. Amazingly, I became alive again. Once the thawing out was complete, I could sense the Spirit's leading in my life.

Is your soul alive today? God's Word says not to worry so much about who can murder your body, but do worry about who or what can murder your soul. Soul murder has eternal consequences.

3. Don't offer your body to sin; offer your body to God.

> [11]In the same way, count yourselves dead to sin but alive to God in Christ Jesus. [12]Therefore do not let sin reign in your mortal body so that you obey its evil desires. [13]Do not offer the parts of your body to sin, as instruments of wickedness, but rather offer yourselves to God, as those who have been brought from death to life; and offer the parts of your body to him as instruments of righteousness. [14]For sin shall not be your master, because you are not under law, but under grace (Romans 6:11–14).

❧ How do you allow sin to reign in your body?

🌿 How have you experienced God delivering you from the sin that once had ruled in your body?

🌿 How can you offer your body as an instrument of righteousness?

You have a choice to make about your body. Without being conscious of this choice, your sin nature will lead you to offer your body to sin. Oh, it may not be hideous sin—not murder, nor theft, nor adultery. But you might just give your mind to television, which interferes with your decision to follow God. Out of boredom or anger you may offer your body to food binges, or allow your tongue to spread gossip, cruelly criticizing or harming others. There are endless ways to allow sin to reign in your body.

Everyone always tells me that I have
such a pretty face—meaning I could
be really pretty if I lost weight.

In place of offering your body to sin, God instructs you to offer your body as an instrument of righteousness. I believe I offer my body as an instrument of righteousness in my church as I lead and participate in prayer. When I dress modestly, my body is an instrument of righteousness. When I use my hands to feed the poor, my body becomes an instrument of righteousness.

See your body as a gift you can give to God. God does not claim you or your body, even though He made you and provides for your very existence. God invites you to dedicate yourself and your body to Him and His will. If you don't give your body to God, it will naturally serve evil. The choice is yours.

4. God gives instructions about how we should treat our bodies and defines sexual sin.

> [3]It is God's will that you should be sanctified: that you should avoid sexual immorality; [4]that each of you should learn to control his own body in a way that is holy and honorable, [5]not in passionate lust like the heathen, who do not know God; [6]and that in this matter no one should wrong his brother or take advantage of him. The Lord will punish men for all such sins, as we have already told you and warned you. [7]For God did not call us to be impure, but to live a holy life. [8]Therefore, he who rejects this instruction does not reject man but God, who gives you his Holy Spirit (1 Thessalonians 4:3–8).

🌿 What instructions does God give about our sexuality in this passage?

🌿 How do we sanctify our bodies?

I read these passages as a teenager and now believe that they give the clearest direction for dealing with sexual standards in dating relationships. Singles are taught that they are not to have sex before marriage, but what about the in-between? How far can you go? According to these passages, you shouldn't be involved in any sexual activity before marriage that would make you feel that you are losing control. Even more than that, if you aren't feeling out of control, it says that you shouldn't be involved in any sexual activity that would cause your partner to lose control. This led me to decide that my sexual standards would be to only hug, hold hands, and kiss before marriage. A standard like that is certainly going against what the world says is okay for young people.

Decisions we make to follow God's standards allow Him to sanctify our bodies. Being sanctified in your body means setting your body apart from the world for God's purposes. I want to encourage you that it is never too late to yield your body to God. Even if you have already been sexually immoral, God promises to forgive you and cleanse you if you confess your sin to Him (1 John 1:9). You can become cleansed from your sexual past and allow God to sanctify you for your sexual future.

5. Your body is temporary.

> ⁶Therefore we are always confident and know that as long as we are at home in the body we are away from the Lord. ⁷We live by faith, not by sight. ⁸We are confident, I say, and would prefer to be away from the body and at home with the Lord. ⁹So we make it our goal to please him, whether we are at home in the body or away from it. ¹⁰For we must all appear before the judgment seat of Christ, that each one may receive what is due him for the things done while in the body, whether good or bad (2 Corinthians 5:6–10).

🌿 While we are at home in the body, we are away from the Lord. Which is better?

🌿 When we appear before the judgment seat, what will we be held accountable for?

It is not bad for you to feel good about being at home in your body. It is most natural for you to want to live here on the earth. You receive comfort from your familiar surroundings. I have lived in Texas for most of my adult life. Since living here, I have witnessed bad weather and heard sirens warning of possible tornadoes in the area. It isn't great to live where there is so much potential to be destroyed by a tornado. But I feel comfortable living here nonetheless. I know what to expect. I know how to take cover. I live on this earth in uncomfortable conditions, yet I have become comfortable with them.

As Paul matured as a Christian, he longed to be in the direct presence of God. He did not fear being away from the body and with the

Lord. He was not suicidal and weary of life and its burdens. He was simply expressing his love and longing to be in Christ's presence. He had actually had some firsthand experience of heaven (2 Corinthians 12:1–4). He did not hate being in the body (except that it meant he couldn't be directly with God). He was happy to remain in his body and away from the Lord in order to complete the tasks God had given him.

When I was a child, my shirt caught on fire and I have unsightly scars on my back. I avoid clothes and events where my scars might show. I even try to hide them from my husband.

When Christians are judged at the judgment seat of Christ described in 2 Corinthians 5:10, we will be judged for what we did while in our bodies. These bodies of ours are like a marker of time. They are in themselves a countdown revealing how much time we have left to serve God on earth. Of course, this isn't the case for all believers. Some children and healthy adults are called home to heaven without any warning from their bodies. The judgment you will receive will be about a specific amount of time—the exact amount of time that you existed in your body.

6. You can glorify God with your body.

> I eagerly expect and hope that I will in no way be ashamed, but will have sufficient courage so that now as always Christ will be exalted in my body, whether by life or by death (Philippians 1:20).

❧ Who do you know who has truly exalted Christ with his or her body whether by life or by death?

His 90th birthday occurred on a Sunday. While his wife and some relatives were home that morning preparing for his birthday celebration, Mr. Cantrell had made a special request of the pastor. Mr. Cantrell had been the president of the Baptist foundation for 22 years. He had faithfully served in our church as a deacon and men's Sunday school teacher, and was even made a deacon for life. On the Sunday of his 90th birthday, he came forward to rededicate whatever years he had left on this earth to serve God. There wasn't a dry eye in the house. What a beautiful way to live in the body.

7. Your body will be transformed in heaven.

> ...who, by the power that enables him to bring every-
> thing under his control, will transform our lowly bodies
> so that they will be like his glorious body (Philippians
> 3:21).

❧ What do you think our bodies will be like when they are glorified like Christ's?

We don't know the answer to this question for sure, but there are clues in Scripture that give us some ideas about our eternal bodies. Jesus moved freely through walls after He rose from the dead (John 20:19).

"Beam me up, Scottie" -style transportation isn't just science fiction. Philip experienced it after he witnessed to the Ethiopian eunuch (Acts 8:39). He was suddenly taken up from the river and appeared in Azotus. Jesus also disappeared (Luke 24:31) and was taken up into heaven (Mark 16:19).

Jesus had a voice that could be recognized (John 20:16), although many times He appeared and wasn't instantly recognized by His outward appearance, but rather by His actions (Luke 24:13–32). We will not have the same desire to marry as we do now (Matthew 22:30). I don't think we will be worried about cellulite or fat cells. Our eternal bodies will be fantastic and freeing at the same time.

8. God instructs us to care for the bodily needs of people we can help.

> [15]Suppose a brother or sister is without clothes and daily
> food. [16]If one of you says to him, "Go, I wish you well;
> keep warm and well fed," but does nothing about his
> physical needs, what good is it? [17]In the same way, faith
> by itself, if it is not accompanied by action, is dead (James
> 2:15–17).

🌿 Should Christians be concerned about the physical needs of
others?

It is always convicting to read Scripture passages like this one in
light of the enormous physical needs that exist in our world today. I
do my little bit, but I know of many more needs than I meet. Sometimes I think, "If we spent only half the time and money we spend on
our beauty regimens on the poor, how many needs would be left?"
Once a month I send just under $30 to Compassion International to
support a needy child. I think of it as my manicure money, even
though I would spend more than that if I got regular manicures every
other week. Do your beauty needs consume you to the point that you
are not even aware of the genuine bodily needs of others?

9. The true healing our bodies need is forgiveness of sins, not a makeover.

> He himself bore our sins in his body on the tree, so that we
> might die to sins and live for righteousness; by his wounds
> you have been healed (1 Peter 2:24).

🌿 How have your wounds been healed by Christ?

It isn't fair, it isn't reasonable, it isn't conceivable, but it is true: I
don't bear my own sins in my body because Jesus Christ bore them for
me on the cross. He bore them so I could be free to die to my sins and

be healed. He was wounded for my healing. We try to heal our body shame by changing our bodies, but that's not where true healing is found.

The most beautiful, perfect Creator of the universe longs to dwell in your body. He wants to live in you. He chooses your body with all its flaws!

Discussion Questions

1. Why doesn't God want us to worry about our bodies?

2. Share ways God meets your bodily needs.

3. How can you glorify God with your body?

4. How does sexual sin affect us differently from other sin?

5. What are some ways you can meet/are meeting the physical needs of others?

6. How is forgiveness of sins a makeover?

CHAPTER FIVE

Biblical Characters Reveal God's View of Beauty

❧

Right after Jesus triumphantly entered Jerusalem riding on a donkey, religious leaders questioned Him in the synagogue. They were attempting to find an excuse to bring charges against Him. When the Sadducees asked Him an incriminating question, Jesus replied, "You are in error because you do not know the Scriptures or the power of God" (Matthew 22:29).

Jesus could say the same to you and me. We are in error when we do not know God's Word or His power. In this chapter, as we dig deep into God's Word, we'll identify what it says about our bodies and our looks, and release the power of God into our lives through His Word.

What can we learn about physical appearances from the Bible? Though the Bible only occasionally mentions a person's appearance in relation to key events in his or her life, we can learn much about God's view of beauty from the lives of Esther, Sarah, Rachel, David, Goliath, Paul, and especially Jesus.

Esther

This short book is an intriguing story of God's protection over His chosen people, the Jews. If you have time you will enjoy reading the whole book. For now, let's look at Esther 2:8, 15, and 17.

> [8]When the king's order and edict had been proclaimed, many girls were brought to the citadel of Susa and put under the care of Hegai. Esther also was taken to the king's palace and entrusted to Hegai, who had charge of the harem.
>
> [15]When the turn came for Esther (the girl Mordecai had adopted, the daughter of his uncle Abihail) to go to the king, she asked for nothing other than what Hegai, the king's eunuch who was in charge of the harem, suggested. And Esther won the favor of everyone who saw her.
>
> [17]Now the king was attracted to Esther more than to any of the other women, and she won his favor and approval more than any of the other virgins. So he set a royal crown on her head and made her queen instead of Vashti.

✎ Was Esther the most beautiful of all the women in the kingdom? (v. 8)

✎ Why was the king more attracted to Esther than to the other women? (vv. 15, 17)

The truth is that Esther possessed physical characteristics that were considered beautiful to the people of that day. However, she wasn't instantly thought to be the most beautiful. When it came to beauty alone there were other qualified contestants. She was attractive enough that the officers, who were instructed to bring the most beautiful virgins to the king's harem, chose Esther to be among the group. Esther was chosen among all of her beautiful peers to be queen for reasons in addition to her physical beauty. She had spent a year in beauty treatments, but her heart and soul had also been nurtured and made beautiful through the years. This was evident by the favor she found with the king and others. The king's eunuch, Hegai, who was in charge of the harem, gave her special secrets that would please the king (Esther 2:15). She wasn't a self-absorbed beauty queen. She understood that true beauty went far beyond the exterior. This is probably what made her most beautiful to the king and the others. Esther's beauty is important to the story only because her physical characteristics first captured the attention of the king.

I'm so fat! I'm about 60 pounds overweight,
and I have tried several diet plans.
They work for a while, but don't last!

Perhaps you know someone like Esther. At first you were most impressed by his or her looks, but as you got to know the person, personality and other character qualities prompted your respect and love.

Sarah
Sarah's beauty is significant during a specific period of her life with Abraham. Genesis 12:10–20 describes her beauty. A portion follows, but if you can, read the entire passage in your Bible.

> [10]Now there was a famine in the land, and Abram went
> down to Egypt to live there for a while because the famine
> was severe. [11]As he was about to enter Egypt, he said to

his wife Sarai, "I know what a beautiful woman you are.
[12]When the Egyptians see you, they will say, 'This is his
wife.' Then they will kill me but will let you live. [13]Say
you are my sister, so that I will be treated well for your
sake and my life will be spared because of you." [14]When
Abram came to Egypt, the Egyptians saw that she was a
very beautiful woman. [15]And when Pharaoh's officials saw
her, they praised her to Pharaoh, and she was taken into
his palace.

❧ Why is Sarah's beauty relevant to what happened in Egypt?

❧ Was Abraham correct in his assumption that Pharaoh
would want to take Sarah as his wife because she was so
beautiful?

Throughout Genesis we learn a lot from the life of Sarah. Personally, I can identify with so much that happens during her spiritual
journey. She wasn't always a flawless example of the life of faith. She
went along with her husband's lies. She came up with a scheme to get
a son for Abraham, and when it backfired, she blamed her husband.
And she laughed at God's message that she would get pregnant at 90-
something. In spite of her shortcomings, she was greatly esteemed by
God for her life of faith. She supported her husband as he followed
God. She nurtured her son Isaac to be a fine man who loved God and
his mother very deeply. She gave her life and trust to God. All of these
characteristics are what made her truly beautiful. In fact, it is these
qualities that God is referring to in 1 Peter 3:5–6. What God found
most beautiful about her was the way she honored her husband.

Her physical beauty is only mentioned in Genesis 12 as an explana-
tion of why Abraham wanted her to lie to the Egyptians and say that she
was his sister. Abraham didn't trust God to protect him. He tried to protect himself, and of course God had to intervene. Sarah was much more
to Abraham than just a pretty woman. She was beautiful according to the

world's standards of beauty in her time, but her true beauty came from her love for and obedience to God. Are you seeking beauty by the standards of the world, or by God's standards? Do you believe you are made more beautiful to God as you love Him and obey Him?

Rachel

Rachel was another Old Testament wife whose beauty is mentioned in Scripture. Jacob fell in love with her at first sight. Their love story is revealed in Genesis 29:16–18.

> [16]Now Laban had two daughters; the name of the older was Leah, and the name of the younger was Rachel. [17]Leah had weak eyes, but Rachel was lovely in form, and beautiful. [18]Jacob was in love with Rachel and said, "I'll work for you seven years in return for your younger daughter Rachel."

How is Rachel's appearance contrasted with her sister's appearance?

How is Rachel's beauty significant to the story?

Jacob saw Rachel and fell deeply in love with her. He thought he was one lucky man. He had just arrived in Paddan Aram, where he was going to hide out from his brother's wrath. He was told to search for a wife among his mother's relatives, and he fell in love with the first woman he met. Jacob was most likely attracted to Rachel because of her beauty. He was utterly shocked that he could be so fortunate to find such a catch among his relatives.

Rachel possessed a beauty that Leah, her sister, didn't measure up to. Laban, Jacob's father-in-law, tricked Jacob into marrying Leah and then struck a deal that required Jacob to work seven more years for Rachel. Rachel and Leah struggled with jealousy all their adult lives. Among the reasons for this jealousy, no doubt, was Rachel's beauty, although there were other factors such as Jacob's favoritism toward Rachel and Rachel's jealousy of Leah's fertility. However, the mention of Rachel's beauty helps us understand the circumstances surrounding the trouble in Jacob's family.

Do you feel jealous of other women's beauty? Statistics reveal that from preschool attractive people receive preferential treatment.

🌿 Is someone else's beauty a problem for you?

🌿 How can you avoid the negative relationship Leah and Rachel experienced?

David

King David's appearance was mentioned after God rebuked Samuel for looking at Jesse's sons' appearance to determine which one should be king. The story is found in 1 Samuel 16:1–13.

> [11]Samuel said, "Send for him; we will not sit down until he arrives." [12]So he sent and had him brought in. He was ruddy, with a fine appearance and handsome features. Then the Lord said, "Rise and anoint him; he is the one" (1 Samuel 16:11b–12).

🌿 Was David handsome?

🌿 Was David's appearance significant to how God wanted to use him to lead the nation of Israel?

As it turns out, David was a pretty handsome guy, a little ruddy, but with a fine appearance. However, on looks alone, Jesse had other sons who seemed more kingly. David wasn't made king until many years later, and he may have developed a more stately, leader-like appearance by then. It is likely that the people followed David as their king partly due to his appearance, but that was only a small part. They understood that Samuel had been told to anoint him as king, and they knew him to be a courageous and fierce warrior.

David's appearance could have gotten in the way of Samuel's assignment (1 Samuel 16:7). God had to instruct Samuel not to choose the son who looked most like a king. On the outside David didn't look like the potential ruler of Israel, but on the inside he was.

My varicose veins make me look like an 80-year-old woman. I try to wear pantyhose all the time, but it isn't easy.

Do you know anyone who did not mature and grow to her full potential because of her physical beauty? Sometimes beautiful people are stunted in their spiritual, emotional, mental, or social growth because they rely only on their physical attractiveness to get by in life and don't develop other qualities. I think this was one of the reasons David didn't look like a king from boyhood. Disguised by his normality, his heart had room to mature extraordinarily.

🌿 How have either your normality or your flaws caused you to develop in the areas mentioned above? Do you think you would have developed in these areas if you were extraordinarily beautiful or had a "perfect" body?

Goliath

Thinking about David's appearance reminds me of Goliath, the giant David battled when still a shepherd boy. Goliath's physical qualities are described in 1 Samuel 17:4–7.

> [4]A champion named Goliath, who was from Gath, came out of the Philistine camp. He was over nine feet tall. [5]He

had a bronze helmet on his head and wore a coat of scale
armor of bronze weighing five thousand shekels; ⁶on his
legs he wore bronze greaves, and a bronze javelin was
slung on his back. ⁷His spear shaft was like a weaver's rod,
and its iron point weighed six hundred shekels. His shield
bearer went ahead of him.

🌿 How tall was Goliath?

🌿 Judging by the armor he wore, how strong do you think
Goliath was?

Goliath was over nine feet tall. He wore heavy armor every day.
Knowing about his size and strength helps us ascertain how intimi-
dating his presence was. Yet David didn't let Goliath's physical attributes intimidate him. He relied on his experiences with God to
determine his actions.

Do you let others' personal appearances intimidate you? How can
you respond to others like David did to Goliath? Are there people you
avoid because they are too attractive or too unattractive? Why not
practice tuning in to God's plan for your relationships rather than
making assumptions about others based on their looks?

Paul

Paul's physical appearance became significant in his relationship with
the church at Corinth. We would probably not know much about
how he looked if he hadn't responded to criticism he received, as
described in 2 Corinthians 10:10–11.

> ¹⁰For some say, "His letters are weighty and forceful, but
> in person he is unimpressive and his speaking amounts to
> nothing." ¹¹Such people should realize that what we are in
> our letters when we are absent, we will be in our actions
> when we are present.

🌿 What were some people saying about Paul?

🌿 What did Paul say about himself?

Evidently, some of Paul's personal characteristics were not all that impressive to some people. Those same people thought he wasn't a great speaker either. Paul didn't let criticism send him to the beauty shop for a makeover. Neither did he sign up for a Toastmasters club. He felt confident that he was following what God had told him to do, and he simply warned the Corinthians that he would bring them God's Truth when he returned to their church.

Jesus

The greatest biblical character we can study to learn about a healthy body image is Jesus Himself. Let's look at John 1:1, 14.

> [1]In the beginning was the Word, and the Word was with God, and the Word was God.
>
> [14]The Word became flesh and made his dwelling among us. We have seen his glory, the glory of the One and Only, who came from the Father, full of grace and truth.

🌿 What did it mean for the Word (Jesus) to become flesh?

Smith and Graybeal state: "In the person of Jesus Christ, God became human, thereby putting his blessing upon the material, physical world in which we live. God as Spirit created a physical body to inhabit—a marvelous, wondrous, indescribable reality harmonizing spirit and matter. By taking on all of the limitation of physical existence and living among us, God told us without words that he loves matter; and because we are made of matter, what we say, what we do, and who we are is invaluable."[1]

Jesus—the Word—was reduced to drool and wet diapers and stomach aches. He allowed Himself to have a complete human experience, with bowel movements and vomit. He didn't create for Himself a souped-up human body. The one He wore would have eventually died (had He not been sacrificed for our sins) like the rest of our bodies. We think we have reasons to dislike our bodies, but Jesus was perfection, and for a time He was flesh! Unlike the rest of us, there is no evidence of body hate in Jesus' life. In fact, we observe just the opposite.

In chapter one we looked at how a healthy body image is characterized by three major components: respect, care, and perspective. There is evidence throughout Jesus' life that He had all three when it came to His body.

The Three Aspects of a Healthy Body Image

Respect

Jesus, as God, spoke the word and all of creation came into being. Jesus has respect for the human body. After all, He was the Creator. Creating something gives you even greater regard for what you have made.

From the time that Brian and I established our first little apartment, I have made the curtains that hang in our homes. I'm not a great seamstress, but I can sew straight lines and that is what is mostly needed for making draperies. And though I am usually eager to rid my home of clutter, in my garage is a box that holds old curtains—from the kitchen curtains I made for our first apartment in Indiana, to the Laura Ashley ones I made for our first house. I don't rush to dump them because they are not just useless pieces of fabric to me. They are a part of my life and the homes I have lived in.

Similarly, we are worth more to Jesus than my curtains are to me. Not only did He have respect for His body, but He also has respect for every body that has come into being. Every body is of incomprehensible value to Him. After all, He came here to die so that all who inhabited those bodies could have eternal life.

Care

I never considered how Jesus cared for His body until I attended a conference for ministers and their spouses at the world-renowned Cooper

Aerobics Center. The conference had identified this special group of caregivers as especially uncaring about their own physical health.

During the conference the speaker began to discuss Jesus and what a healthy person He was. Of course, he had to point out that Jesus was aerobically fit. He had evidence to back up his claims. He measured the miles between cities that Jesus walked in His three years of open ministry and calculated that Jesus was in peak aerobic fitness. He also took into consideration that Jesus had been a carpenter and lumber-jack, occupations that would have given him high levels of muscular endurance, strength, and flexibility. He considered the typical Mediterranean diet rich in nuts, figs, fruits, and grains, and the fact that Jesus often fed others a nutritious meal of broiled fish and whole-grain bread. He determined that Jesus ate in a healthful manner. He also noted that an unhealthy body couldn't have endured the scourging and emotional trauma Jesus went through. It was because Jesus took such care of His body that He could stay alive all the way to the cross, in order to fulfill God's plan (John 3:14).[2]

Perspective

Jesus' physical attributes were prophesied in Isaiah 53:2.

> He grew up before him like a tender shoot, and like a root
> out of dry ground. He had no beauty or majesty to attract
> us to him, nothing in his appearance that we should
> desire him.

🌿 What purpose do you suppose God had in giving Jesus a body that had no beauty or majesty to attract people to Him?

Although the most popular paintings of Jesus are the blue-eyed, beautiful Jesus of the Renaissance painters, those paintings are far from accurate in portraying how Jesus looked. Being Jewish, it is more likely that Jesus' skin was darker than depicted, and He probably had brown eyes and dark hair. He may have had a big nose, and though

His body was well cared for, He wouldn't have been known for His pecs and washboard abs. His hands were probably callused and scarred from His years of work as a carpenter. There was nothing about His outward appearance to draw people to Him, but His inner kindness, confidence, and love attracted thousands to His side.

My hair is a frizzball. I hate rainy or humid days because I look like I have a huge ball of tangled yarn attached to the top of my head.

Jesus had perspective in all of this. He didn't want to come to earth in a body that was the ultimate in human perfection. He came to the earth to show the extravagance of God's love, not to get distracted by things that don't last for eternity.

🌿 Was Jesus beautiful?

🌿 Why do you think God didn't give Jesus the best physical qualities that exist?

Physical beauty just isn't that important to God. Evidently, God thought it was important to make Jesus average in appearance. He didn't want people following Jesus because He was handsome. However, humans can't resist incorporating their ideas of beauty when they paint, draw, and illustrate Jesus.

🌿 How would you imagine Jesus to look based on Isaiah 53:2?

I think of Jesus as a short, balding, skinny, dark-eyed, dark-haired, olive-skinned man with crooked teeth and a big nose. And I totally love Him. I've never seen Jesus, but I love Him because of Who He is.

In Revelation 1, John records his experience of seeing a now-reigning Christ. John had been very close to Jesus when He lived on the earth. John saw Jesus at the Transfiguration (Matthew 17:1–13), and on the cross (John 19:26–27). He saw Him risen from the dead and was the first to recognize Him (John 21:7), but he never reacted to Jesus the way he did when he saw Him in Revelation 1.

> [13]And among the lampstands was someone "like a son of man," dressed in a robe reaching down to his feet and with a golden sash around his chest. [14]His head and hair were white like wool, as white as snow, and his eyes were like blazing fire. [15]His feet were like bronze glowing in a furnace, and his voice was like the sound of rushing waters. [16]In his right hand he held seven stars, and out of his mouth came a sharp double-edged sword. His face was like the sun shining in all its brilliance. [17]When I saw him, I fell at his feet as though dead. Then he placed his right hand on me and said: "Do not be afraid. I am the First and the Last. [18]I am the Living One; I was dead, and behold I am alive for ever and ever! And I hold the keys of death and Hades."

❧ How did John respond to seeing Jesus?

❧ Are you drawn to this image?

I am not yet completely comfortable with this image of Jesus. The first time I read that passage, it didn't make me feel close to Him. I could understand why John felt so afraid and fainted as a dead man when he viewed Jesus this way. But I trust God's Word that when I see clearly I will be drawn to that image of Jesus. Even now, as I read over the passage and recognize that this image of the conquering Jesus is also mandatory in order for God's good plan to be accomplished, I appreciate Jesus' appearance more. He is a picture of the conquering hero, dressed for battle. He won over sin when His bruised and bleeding flesh hung on a cross. He comes to set the world straight when He returns again in total and complete victory—eyes blazing like fire, hair white as wool, legs of bronze, dressed in linen and gold. He is the King! He is my King. His victory is my victory. I am safe when I am close to Him.

If you will allow the truth of God's Word to unleash its power in your life, you will accept His value of you. Your appearance isn't all that important to God. God cares about your love and obedience. God doesn't show His love and favor by giving you beauty or withholding it from you. Beauty does not have the importance for God that it has in our world.

Discussion Questions

1. How much emphasis does the Bible place on people's physical characteristics?

2. Why was Esther chosen to be Queen of Persia—her beauty or her character?

3. Why did God tell us about Sarah's physical beauty? Why isn't her beauty mentioned the first time we are told about her?

4. Why did Jesus need a body?

5. How did Jesus demonstrate respect, care, and perspective for His body?

6. How was David's appearance significant to Samuel anointing him as king?

CHAPTER SIX

Transforming Your Mind, Transforming Your Body Image

Laurie's double mastectomy with reconstructive surgery took place without major complications. Recovery was difficult and included chemotherapy, but here she sat two years after her last chemo treatment, her hair grown back in a texture and color she hardly recognized, glad to be alive. She'd just received good news from her doctor, and her life had taken on a sense of normalcy again.

Laurie hadn't been focusing on her disfigured body as much as she had been concerned with just staying alive. The good news that her cancer was in remission allowed her to stop and consider the body she was left with in the aftermath of cancer.

How did she love and accept this body? In one sense she felt betrayed by it. In another sense she was just like everyone else, feeling ashamed of her scars, unnatural shape, an extra layer of fat, varicose veins, and all. In the scope of two years her normal body flaws had transformed into massive alterations (in her opinion). But after what she had been through, she would never consider optional surgery to correct any of these body flaws. So what was she supposed to do now?

Making Peace with Your Body Starts with What You Believe

Laurie needed to start confronting the lies she believed about herself. A healthy body image starts in transforming the mind. What you think about your body is your body image. If you think negatively about your body, then you have a negative body image. If you think positively about your body, you have a healthy body image. A healthy body image has no correlation to what you weigh or how you look.

I feel pressure to look as good as all the other doctors' wives.
I don't have time to know if I really like how I look,
I'm so busy trying to look better.

You do not have direct control over your feelings, but you do have control over what you think and how you behave. These next two chapters will help you discover new ways to think and act toward your body. God's Word challenges you to be transformed in your mind. You don't need a body makeover; you need a mind makeover.

Mind Makeover

Recent research has pinpointed the specific part of the brain that controls your sense of self and body image.[1] The study shows how front temporal dementia causes individuals to change their political or religious beliefs, the type of clothes they wear, foods they like, and more. This research confirms the importance of making over your mind and the power of your thoughts over the rest of your life.

In Matthew 16, Jesus rebuked Peter for not having the right mind-set. After Jesus predicted His upcoming death, Peter responded, "This shall never happen to you" (Matthew 16:22).

"Jesus turned and said to Peter, 'Get behind me, Satan! You are a stumbling block to me; you do not have in mind the things of God, but the things of men' " (Matthew 16:23).

It is very important to survey what thoughts guide your life. Do you have in mind the things of God, or the things of men? What you have in mind will make a big difference in how you live and enjoy your life. You may be surprised to find how much your mind is influenced by the world when it comes to beauty.

> [1]Therefore, I urge you, brothers, in view of God's mercy, to offer your bodies as living sacrifices, holy and pleasing to God—this is your spiritual act of worship. [2]Do not conform any longer to the pattern of this world, but be transformed by the renewing of your mind. Then you will be able to test and approve what God's will is—his good, pleasing and perfect will (Romans 12:1–2).

✺ What are you not supposed to do according to this passage? What are you asked to do?

If your desire is to accept and use your body the way God's Word instructs, it is clear from this passage that you will be going against the tide of the world. God gave you your body. He invites you to offer it back to Him as a living sacrifice. God is not interested in human sacrifices as the pagan gods are—literally giving your body to be burned or consumed. Rather, God asks you to live in your body (living sacrifice), yet to live in your body for God's glory not your own (sacrifice). If you have been moved by God's marvelous mercy toward you, you can respond in love by giving your life (which includes your body) to Him. Dedicating your entire life to God is pleasing to Him.

How do you live your life as a living sacrifice? You do this by renewing your mind. You do not conform to the pattern of the world.

You allow God to work in you, and you believe the things that God tells you are the truth, rather than what the world tells you. You replace your old belief system, which is based on the world's philosophies, with God's Word. As my good friend Ron Rand says, "You've got to get the L out!" When he says this to an audience they do a double take to make sure they heard him right. It sounds like another phrase and gets their attention. It makes the point well, though. You need to get the "L" out and stop worrying what the *world* says; rather, center your life on what the *Word* says.

If you listen to the world, you are only valuable if you wear the latest style of clothing over a perfect body. If you listen to the Word, you are valuable when you wear the clothes that fit into your budget over a body that contains a heart that loves and lives for God.

Let's look at what the world tells us versus what the truth is when it comes to common body-image myths.

Seven Lies the World Tells About Our Bodies

1. If I change something about my body, I will finally like myself.
Just get up early on a weekend morning and start clicking through the cable television channels, and you will see how pervasive this message is. Whatever bothers you about your appearance, a product exists to fix it for five easy installments of $49.99. These television infomercials provide solid testimonials of women and men whose lives have been changed by "amazing" products. Though the products may vary, the story is always the same: These people went from suffering low self-esteem to feeling on top of the world after they used these products to diet, enlarge breasts, replace hair, remove unwanted hair, clear up acne, erase wrinkles, trim waists, firm thighs, and so on.

Think about this for yourself. If you could purchase a product (that you could afford) that would change the _____ (part of your body that you dislike most), would it raise your self-esteem? I acknowledge that people do feel a little better about themselves after they receive positive feedback about something they have changed, such as losing weight. But the positive feelings don't last long.

Your self-esteem isn't as much about how you look right now as it is about what you *think* about how you look right now. Consider the following illustration from Jane's life.

Jane went on a fad diet and quickly lost 50 pounds. After the first 25 were gone, people started to notice and say positive things to Jane. By the time she lost all 50 (in four months), several of her friends noticed and wanted to know what she was doing. It felt awesome to know she was an example for others. Tim, a man Jane had worked with for a long time and greatly admired, asked her for a date after she had lost 50 pounds. She couldn't have been happier. She knew that he would never have asked her when she was heavier, and she didn't mind. She believed that she was worthy of him now that she was skinny. It seemed as if Jane's self-esteem had totally changed.

I was born with a cleft lip, and although surgery
has fixed it, I still feel a little like a freak.

The night of the date, Tim called and canceled. He said he was sick. Jane didn't believe him. She knew that he had seen her in the break room eating a small piece of chocolate birthday cake. She believed that he canceled the date because he began to doubt that getting involved with her was a wise thing. She assumed that he thought she would gain back all the weight and she couldn't stay thin. Even though Jane had lost the 50 pounds and eating the piece of cake didn't affect her weight at all, she returned to being the same self-loathing person she had been before her diet. The increase in self-esteem was shallow and temporary. Nothing of substance had changed in the way Jane saw herself.

Jane found out later that Tim really had been sick. He was out of work the whole next week with the flu. Jane realized through this experience that changing her body was not enough to change her self-esteem problems. She still felt just as bad about herself, if not worse.

The truth: Healthy self-esteem comes from believing in the value God holds of you, not in the value man places in you.

> ❧ Check yourself:
> Do you believe that even if you changed _____ (whatever you dislike most about your body) you could still dislike yourself?

2. My outward appearance is the most important thing about me. Proverbs 11:22 says, "Like a gold ring in a pig's snout is a beautiful woman who shows no discretion."

It is part of human development for adolescents to become overly preoccupied with their physical appearance, but some women never move beyond this developmental stage. You recognize it in their closets. The overabundance of clothes shows the emphasis they put on appearances. Their checkbooks reveal their insecurities about their looks.

In chapter three you tallied the amount of time you spend on your looks. Was it a reasonable amount of time? Could you spend less time on your appearance? Are you unable to make a change because you believe this statement to be true: "How I look is the most important thing about me"?

Here's an assignment for you: Go to the grocery store or some other public place without makeup on and without your hair done. Another recommendation is to fast from buying new clothes, makeup, or other beauty products for three months. (Don't go on a shopping spree before you do this, either.) Wear last year's bathing suit. Use up some of the beauty products that are cluttering your bathroom drawers and cabinets.

Surviving breast cancer helped Laurie realize that her health is more important than her appearance. She may not like everything about the way her body was changed by surgery and chemo, but she's glad she has more days left on the earth, and she wants to live them free of despair about her body.

The truth: Your outward appearance is what people will first judge you by, but your personality, self-confidence, talents and abilities, and your spiritual sensitivity are each vital to who you are as well.

� Check yourself:
Do you think it is wrong for people to accept or reject you on the basis of your appearance alone?

3. Everyone can look like movie stars or fashion models if they diet enough and work at it enough. Jeanine had been bulimic since her twenties. It started in college when she threw up regularly in order to have a flat stomach for spring break. It turned into a 13-year habit that consumed her life. She can still recall how she felt about her body back then. Basically, she felt attractive and healthy. The only thing she didn't like was the little ring of fat that encircled her abdomen. She read a magazine article about a top fashion model that included pictures of the model working out and wearing a bikini revealing a totally flat stomach. The article convinced her that if she followed this model's diet and exercise plan she could have a perfectly flat stomach too.

Jeanine believed it. She believed she could have a flat stomach, and she believed that she *should* have a flat stomach. But with spring break just around the corner, she forced herself to vomit as a faster path to movie-star results. After she threw up, Jeanine was convinced that her stomach was flatter. So she kept on and on and hasn't stopped since, although she has often tried.

People develop eating disorders for many reasons. In Jeanine's case, although there were other contributing factors, there's no doubt that she honestly believed she could make her stomach look like the model's and that she ought to do so.

When Jeanine and I talked, I asked her to bring in pictures of her relatives. She had been to a family reunion on her mother's side recently, so we looked over a group picture of aunts and uncles, cousins and siblings. About half of those in the picture had similar body types. None were tall and lanky (like the model). Most of the women were between 5'3" and 5'6". They were average in weight. All of the women had a little more plumpness around their stomach area. Jeanine knew for a fact that most of them didn't eat right or exercise, but her Aunt Jenny, who was 65 at the time the picture was taken, had been a gym teacher and was a picture of health all her life. When we zeroed in on Aunt Jenny, whom Jeanine never considered fat, she could see the little bit of plumpness in her stomach area too. This helped Jeanine face the fact that she could not have the flat stomach of the famous model, even after 13 years of throwing up. All bulimia had given her was a mixed-up metabolism and rotting teeth. At 33, her stomach was rounder than it had ever been and she was in terrible health.

It will be helpful for you to take a good long look at the genetic makeup you inherited. Look at your blood relatives and observe any dominant body characteristics that you have in common. Develop a realistic expectation of the body that is healthy for you by considering pictures of relatives rather than movie stars.

Those of us who are 40 and older have a greater advantage in look-ing at our relatives to get a better grasp of how our bodies are supposed to look. Generations before ours seldom tortured and mistreated their bodies on a quest for thinness. For the younger generation, though, this exercise may prove more difficult. Some of your relatives may have distorted their body shape through eating disorders, surgery, and chronic dieting. On the other hand, you may have relatives who have abused their bodies through obesity. This doesn't mean that you should just give in and do the same. You can recognize the genetic pre-disposition you may have toward obesity and work toward keeping your body healthy in spite of it.

Here's another helpful exercise for you: Get out photo albums and look at pictures of your blood relatives. Record your answers to the following questions in your journal.

    ❧ How is your body shape similar to that of your relatives?

    ❧ How is your body different from that of your relatives?

❦ What is most natural for you to expect your body to look like if you consider the characteristics you see in these family pictures and in yourself?

❦ What is the best look for your body if you take good care of it?

The truth: We will tend to look more like our blood relatives than movie stars and models.

❦ Check yourself:
Do you believe that you can't and you shouldn't have to look like a movie star or model?

4. Attractive people don't have any problems. The only thing Stella wanted in life was to be attractive. She'd felt ugly and inferior in high school. During college and into her first job, she lost weight and learned how to style her hair and wear makeup in an attractive way. People who knew her in high school were bowled over at their five-year reunion. She had literally been transformed.

Stella had wanted to look this way all through her high school years. The main reason she wanted to look good was so she wouldn't have to feel the pain of loneliness anymore. In high school when she saw the pretty and popular cheerleaders, she thought their lives were perfect. She envied them. But looking like a cheerleader wasn't the answer to her problems. In fact, the closer Stella got to being accepted by the type of girls she'd always envied, the more she realized that their problems were just as bad as, if not worse than, her own.

The truth is that we all have problems. Some of our problems can be made worse because of appearance. Often, more is expected of attractive people. It is true, on the other hand, that less attractive people have been discriminated against. If you think improving your appearance will make all your troubles go away you are kidding yourself. You may be less troubled by your appearance, but you still must face the same amount of pressure and difficulty that you did before.

The truth: We all have troubles in this life, and being attractive doesn't make you immune to problems.

    🌿 Check yourself:

> Do you believe that even if you changed your body flaws the way you wanted to you would still feel pain and have troubles?

5. Being overweight is a sin. Remember Christine from earlier chapters? She is the one who, although overweight, was honored to be asked to take part in the church fashion show. Her response was a direct contrast to Marybeth's, who looked more the model type than Christine did. Marybeth immediately refused because she hated her body so much.

Christine didn't come to that place of peace about her body easily. She got there only through the love and support she found in her relationship with God. One area that seemed to block her closeness to God was her disgust with her fat. She believed she was a Christian, but she felt she was a bad one since she couldn't keep her weight under control. Christine transferred her mom's feelings about her weight to God. She automatically thought that God hated her being fat, even though He accepted her as His child. She didn't try to get close to God because she felt she was an embarrassment to Him.

I can't even find my waist anymore.

So, what changed? How did Christine become so accepting of herself? It started one day in the church kitchen when she and Lydia were preparing a meal for the senior citizens' luncheon. Christine and Lydia were laughing and joking as they cooked and cleaned. Then something slipped out of Christine's mouth that would change her life forever. She confessed as she was putting the chocolate frosting on the cake, "I know it's a sin to like frosting as much as I do, but God's just gonna have to look the other way."

Lydia's response was far from what Christine expected. She looked puzzled and asked, "Why do you think it's a sin to like chocolate frosting?" Christine was so astonished she couldn't formulate an answer. She stammered out something about her mom and God hating fat, and a couple of other reasons.

That was the first time Christine was ever challenged to think that God wasn't as concerned about her losing weight as her mother was. Christine's real sin wasn't liking chocolate, it was turning to food for needs that only God could meet. Through developing a more personal relationship with God, she discovered that she was missing out on much courage, strength, and intimacy because of her fear that God rejected her body (as everybody else in her life did). Once she came to see herself as fully accepted by God even if she gained 50 pounds, she started to see her body differently.

The result of growing closer to God is a new desire to care more for the body God gave her. But she is choosing to care for her body in a totally different way than she did in the past. She isn't going on some kind of crash diet. Actually, she found a prayer-walking partner in Lydia, and together they walk around the church and neighborhood three times a week praying for their families and their community. She is also making better choices about the food she consumes. She doesn't deny herself chocolate; rather, she is relying on God to help her in her goal of having one chocolate dessert each week. Even when she gives in and eats too much chocolate, she knows that God is on her side. Christine is losing weight ever so slowly. The best thing is that she is doing it in the freedom of acceptance by Christ and the power of His love.

The truth: It is not a sin to be overweight. The real sin for many heavy (or skinny) people is turning to food (or other substances) to meet needs only God can meet.

❧ Check yourself:
> Do you think God doesn't consider your weight when it comes to His love for you?

6. I must compete with other women and look as good as they do.
Cindy was packing for the Holy Land tour she was attending with her church. Her thoughts automatically turned to the best dressers from the group. She guessed what clothes these women would wear and tried to gauge what to take based on how she would look compared to them, rather than what would be most comfortable and wrinkle the least.

Have you ever done the same thing? When you think about what to wear, do you think, "What will the other women be wearing?" Are there women you want to out-dress, or at least dress up to their standards?

I'm 30 and I have never been in a serious relationship with a man. I'm sure that my looks have everything to do with that.

You don't achieve self-worth by looking as good as or better than other women. Women who struggle in this area often notice only the women who are more attractive than they are anyway. The practice only leads them to bring to light more body flaws. There will always be women who are prettier or less attractive than you are. That is a given. When you accept this reality you are free to think about more important things.

The truth: You will always be the loser when you compete for beauty with other women.

❧ Check yourself:
> Do you believe that you are more attractive than some women and less attractive than others?

7. My body is who I am. When did Adam's body come to life? Not the instant it was created. It was lifeless until God breathed into his nostrils the breath of life. Will your body last forever? No, but you will exist eternally either in heaven or hell depending on whether you receive God's free gift of salvation through Jesus Christ. I like to think of our bodies as the garage of our souls. It is where we are parked temporarily while we live on this earth. The health, appearance, and abilities of our bodies do affect what we do on this earth, but they are not all of who we are. They are significant to us for our time on earth, but will not last for eternity.

The truth: Your body is part of who you are, but not completely who you are.

❧ Check yourself:
   Do you recognize that you exist much deeper than your body?

Read back over your answers and check yourself. Each question that you answer no to indicates that you are believing a lie about yourself. Write down the truth in contrast to the lie and put the list somewhere you will see it often (taped to the bathroom mirror, sitting on your dresser, on your car dashboard). Each time you read the truth, ask God to help you believe it.

What about the Change?

The world says that which can be measured and observed is what gives you value. If your figure and looks are consistent with the world's view of beauty, then you are considered valuable. As you saw in Romans 12:1–2, you must be transformed from the world's thinking. It is the Holy Spirit who shows you God's will and gives you God's power when you come out of the world's pattern. The Holy Spirit does an invisible work that transforms your body image.

> ⁶We do, however, speak a message of wisdom among the mature, but not the wisdom of this age or of the rulers of

this age, who are coming to nothing. [7]No, we speak of God's secret wisdom, a wisdom that has been hidden and that God destined for our glory before time began. [8]None of the rulers of this age understood it, for if they had, they would not have crucified the Lord of glory (1 Corinthians 2:6–8).

❧ What is the wisdom of this age when it comes to body image?

❧ What is God's secret wisdom?

❧ How many of the models, movie makers, and advertisers of this age who promote the "perfect American body" recognize Jesus Christ as the Son of God? Can they possess real wisdom if they don't?

The wisdom of this age says that you are not worthy unless you look like you are 23 and have large, perky breasts and no body fat. This is not very wise when you consider that our bodies weren't created to have that shape, and most of us eventually live past the age of 23. The majority of the actresses and models who do look like that are abusing their bodies through surgery and starvation. God's secret wisdom is that *every body is beautiful!*

We are each unique and special. We may not win the approval of the world for how we look, but true wisdom comes from experiencing the reality that most of what the world offers is untrue. God tells you that you can have peace in your soul no matter what your body looks like. The world offers you peace if you look a certain way. Does that peace ever come? Have you ever found true, deep, and spiritual peace when you looked your best? Are Hollywood filmmakers, advertisers, and the fashion industry centered on a meaningful relationship with God when they feed us beliefs about what it means to be beautiful? True beauty is experienced as you bask in the center of God's love and care for you—all of you—spirit, body, and soul.

Putting It into Practice

🌿 Write down three negative statements you make about your body. Go back and rewrite them as positive statements by using some of the information in this chapter.

Here's what Laurie wrote in her journal:

1. My scars are ugly and I'm disfigured.
2. My stomach is too round.
3. My varicose veins are hideous.

It was difficult for her to be more realistic, but when she was, she wrote:

1. I am not happy with the fact that I had to have a mastectomy, but I'm glad that it was successful in getting rid of my cancer. I will accept it when my husband tells me I am just as sexy to him now as before.
2. Most women have an extra layer of fat across their abdomens. My stomach is here to stay.
3. My veins have gotten worse since I had cancer. I can look at them and celebrate that I am alive!

In a *Guideposts* magazine story, Fay Angus wrote about an experience she had. She told how she guided her children to have prayer time at the dinner table. She saw this as a time for her children to learn to be comfortable about praying out loud, develop the gift of gratefulness, and speak freely with God. She writes:

> One evening when shepherd's pie, the children's favorite, was on the table, six-year-old Ian enthusiastically volunteered to say the blessing. After he had duly thanked God for the food and the highlights of his day, he paused and then added, "And thank You, God, for the nice little boy You gave this family."
>
> "Nice little boy!" I gasped. "Where?"
>
> "Right here," he grinned, pointing to himself. "I was thanking God for me!"

Doing the dishes later that night, I thought, the boy has a point. We all come tagged with the designer label: "Individually Crafted With the Compliments of Your Creator." Suddenly I was overwhelmed. Why, in all my years of thanksgiving, I had never ever thanked God for me! Hands dripping wet with suds, eyes spilling tears of wonder, then and there I quietly said, "Thank You, God, for all the workmanship You put into making me!"[2]

Why not follow the example of a six year old and thank God for making you?

Discussion Questions

1. How do you have to treat the world's way of thinking about body image if you are going to be transformed into God's way of thinking about your body? (See Romans 12:1–2.)

2. Which of the seven lies do you struggle with most often?

3. Do you struggle to see God as accepting and loving you even if you are overweight and eat compulsively?

4. If we can't all look like movie stars, what should we strive for in our appearance?

5. Why is it magical thinking to believe that if we looked better, our problems would go away?

6. How does the Holy Spirit work to transform your body image?

CHAPTER SEVEN

Feeling Beautiful: Transforming Your Feelings about Your Body

When you don't like your body, thoughts and feelings of contempt pour over you. You look down at your stomach in the
shower and your whole being cringes in shame. You are overcome by
disgust and hopelessness. The despair you feel is tightly tied to your
sense of who you are. You think that who you are is wrong. You try to
bury your feelings, but they materialize throughout your day. As you
finish your last bite at lunch and notice that your waistband is tight,
you berate yourself a little more. When you're alone at home and all
you can think about is the gallon of your favorite ice cream in the
freezer, you think, "Why deny myself? My stomach is fat and ugly
anyway."

Most women experience these feelings as mild shame, and they are
able to function when not distracted by occasional negative thoughts

and feelings. But others are trapped in "Bodyhateville" perpetually. They are overcome by guilt, shame, disgust, hopelessness, and anger with each bite of food they put into their mouths. Every glance in the mirror and each person who looks at them reflect reproach and condemnation. Feelings can literally crush your spirit. Negative feelings about your body hinder you from receiving the life God wants for you.

Read the following scriptures from Proverbs and answer the questions with these verses in mind.

> A happy heart makes the face cheerful, but heartache crushes the spirit (Proverbs 15:13).
>
> A cheerful heart is good medicine, but a crushed spirit dries up the bones (Proverbs 17:22).
>
> A man's spirit sustains him in sickness, but a crushed spirit who can bear? (Proverbs 18:14)
>
> The lamp of the Lord searches the spirit of a man; it searches out his inmost being (Proverbs 20:27).

🌿 How much damage can negative feelings (a crushed spirit) cause in your life?

🌿 Why is it important to address these negative feelings rather than push them away?

Women are emotional creatures. We are usually much more in touch with our feelings than our male counterparts. This is something women like about themselves—that they can identify their feelings and express them to others. A woman's ability to be sensitive to her own and others' feelings brings a positive aspect to her relationships.

The emotional nature of women is highlighted at the central point in history, during Jesus' journey to the cross. Even though Jewish law forbade showing compassion for condemned prisoners, a group of women caught sight of their Savior being brutalized and responded by weeping (Luke 23:27–31). Henry Gariepy writes, "With all the record of opposition to Jesus, there is no instance written of in which a woman opposed Christ. No women ever forsook, betrayed, or in any way expressed enmity against Christ. Rather they followed Him, opened to Him their homes and hearts, bathed His feet with their tears, anointed His head with perfume, and now, as men dragged Him to His death, they showed the compassion of their sorrow and wept for Him on His way to martyrdom."[1]

Women can be proud of their emotionally sensitive natures. It is a God-given gift and capacity. This compassion was appropriate for Christ's circumstances on the cross, and in the midst of it, Jesus acknowledges the emotional state of the women. Jesus made the longest recorded statement on His journey to the cross in His address to these precious women.

> [28]Jesus turned and said to them, "Daughters of Jerusalem, do not weep for me; weep for yourselves and for your children. [29]For the time will come when you will say, 'Blessed are the barren women, the wombs that never bore and the breasts that never nursed!' [30]Then 'they will say to the mountains, "Fall on us!" and to the hills, "Cover us!" ' [31]For if men do these things when the tree is green, what will happen when it is dry?" (Luke 23:28–31)

🌺 What did Jesus instruct the women to do in this passage?

Jesus didn't scold them for weeping, He merely told them that what they were weeping about was a waste of their time. It was only natural for them to weep. Their leader, friend, healer, and guide was being brutally battered. This was indeed a sad scene. But the truth is that this ugly event did not take into account spiritual reality. The spiritual reality was that God was in control. Jesus' barbaric death was necessary and it fulfilled God's plan. If the women had understood what was actually happening, they wouldn't have needed tears of sorrow. Jesus went on to instruct them about what they should weep about. They did need to weep because their whole city and temple would be destroyed. That prophecy was fulfilled in A.D. 70.

I think Jesus says something similar to you and me. "Don't weep (feel negative emotions) about your physical body that God gave to you for your earthly existence and which will not last for eternity. Weep (feel negative emotions) about issues that are of true consequence. Weep for the unsaved, for the hurting and confused. You are wasting your tears weeping about your body."

How Women Deal with Negative Feelings

Identifying feelings can bog women down when they don't know what to do with them. When it comes to negative feelings about their bodies, women usually respond in one of two ways: They either try to stuff their feelings, or they try to change their feelings by changing their bodies. Neither brings peace and harmony to their emotions.

Marjorie is a feelings-stuffer. Marjorie is overweight. She gained about 20 pounds with each of her three children, so she would need to lose 60 pounds to get back down to her pre-pregnancy weight (a weight she would love to weigh now, but at the time thought was too heavy).

Since the birth of her first child, Marjorie has been stuffing her feelings of dislike for her body. The year after her child's birth, she told herself that the extra weight was normal since she was nursing. She tried to believe that it didn't bother her. The few comments that her husband made about her weight made her angry. She thought that he was an insensitive man who didn't know what it was like for a woman having babies. A few times she agreed to a new exercise program with a neighbor, but she did it more for the fellowship than for her health. When it rained or was too hot or too cold and the exercise dates fizzled out, she discovered different ways to fellowship. She had her friends over for dessert and coffee.

Marjorie didn't let herself feel ugly, fat, and unhealthy for long. She quickly changed her emotions by stuffing them away. If you had asked her directly, "How do you feel about your body?" she would have responded, "I feel great, I can eat all the ice cream I want without guilt." The truth is she had a great deal of guilt. In fact, she was overwhelmed with guilt, low self-esteem, and emptiness. She secretly hated skinny people and couldn't trust them or anything they said. She covered all these negative feelings with her addictions to food, decorating, and television.

I've tried about everything, but there is no way to change the shape of my thunder thighs. Running just makes them bigger!

While Marjorie appeared indifferent to any negative feelings about her body, Jana was obsessed with negative feelings almost 24 hours a day. She couldn't have one mellow moment without thinking about how ugly a certain part of her body was. It didn't help that she was a ballerina by profession and danced in front of a mirror while teaching and practicing. That mirror haunted her. Several times a day she was so overwhelmed by the image she saw that she lost concentration and had to work extra hard to get back on task.

Can you imagine feeling constantly criticized by the image you saw in the mirror eight hours a day? Jana couldn't escape it. Even while driving from work to the dance studio where she taught, she was confronted by the rearview mirror. Her whole life centered on acknowledging, resisting, and being tormented by debilitating and negative feelings. She felt bad, but it was so much easier for her to hate her thighs than to acknowledge her hurt and anger toward the important people in her life.

The Power of Emotions

Emotions are a very powerful impetus in your life. Your emotions may not be driving you to the same extremes as Marjorie or Jana. You may be somewhere in between. Just as emotions wield a strong negative power, when they are based on truth, they become powerful sources of energy and life. I like this description of emotions by Flora Slosson Wuellner:

> No matter how distorted and hurtful our powers within, they were originally created from the divine source, and they hold the potentiality for the unique and beautiful. In their healing, they are not wiped out or destroyed, for nothing in God's creation can ultimately be destroyed. Rather, they are restored to their original, intended power of gifted creativity.
>
> Our fear, when healed, becomes intuitive, empathetic compassion and sensitivity toward others.
>
> Our destructive anger, when healed, becomes a passion, a hunger and thirst for justice and righteousness.
>
> Our perfectionism, our compulsion to organize and dominate, when healed, becomes released, joyous power to build and create.
>
> Our inertia and our withdrawals, when healed, become increasing powers of peace and integrity.
>
> Our possessiveness, our jealousies, and our physical addictions, when healed, become growing released powers to become lovers and healers of the world around us.[2]

Are you willing to let God heal you from your negative emotions?

How have your negative emotions robbed you in this life?

There is a sense in which you must give consent to God for the healing of emotions to begin. God longs to heal you; He promises to heal you. Wuellner says, "But God's full healing seems to wait for our longing and consent. Is this because we are not helpless puppets but created to be children, heirs, spouses, partners, co creators with God, our free consent a crucial part of the creative wisdom of gravity."[3]

When the overwhelming feelings of a negative body image are healed, they turn into wonder and awe at the body God gave each of us. While we respect the limitations our bodies may have compared to others, we value every muscle that we have and every movement we are blessed to make. We turn self-hate into praise for the Creator who made us.

Truth Heals Your Emotions

You've already laid the groundwork for healing your emotions in the previous chapters. From the Bible you have been digging out the truth of who you are and why God made you. When you believe this truth, it will positively affect your feelings. Again, you do not have direct control over your feelings. You *do* have direct control over how you think and what you do.

My dad told me that guys won't marry fat girls.

It is similar to how your heart functions in your body. Your heart works on an automatic response system. It started beating when you were only a few days past conception and won't stop until physical limitations completely inhibit its ability to operate. In your day-to-day existence, you do not have direct control over your heartbeat. You can take a short jog and it will beat a little faster. You can rest and it will slow down. You simply can't tell your heart how and when to beat. Yet you do have some control over the health of your heart through diet and exercise.

It is the same with your feelings. Feelings are automatic responses to what we think about our circumstances. We do not change our feelings by simply saying "I don't feel that way." However, we can control our feelings by controlling how we think.

If you are searching for emotional freedom from negative feelings about your body, you need to discover how to address your feelings in a healthy way. The following is a guide for dealing with your feelings.

Step One: Identify your feelings. Although Marjorie (the mother of three) appears the happiest of our previous two examples, actually Jana (the ballerina) is closer to healing from her emotional deficiencies. Marjorie totally ignores her feelings. She stuffs them down deep by piling on activities and an "I couldn't care less about looking good" attitude in an attempt to keep them in the grave. Jana is the one who is totally obsessed and overcome by negative feelings. However, she will more likely recognize that she needs help handling her negative feelings.

Our negative feelings signal that something is wrong. All feelings are real, but not all feelings are true. For instance, you may feel ugly, disgusting, and worthless. Those are real feelings. But you are God's beloved creation, and as such, you are beautiful, appealing, and worth more than gold. You first have to be able to identify your feelings before you can discover the *truth* that will change your feelings.

  Write down any negative feelings you can identify that describe how you feel about your body right now. Here are some to get you started, but you may have others:

angry	anxious	hopeless
sad	embarrassed	disgusted
tense	worried	gloomy
ashamed	guilty	dejected
discouraged	unhappy	repulsive
vain	self-effacing	arrogant
haughty	lowly	gross
hideous	forbidding	ugly
self-conscious		

❧ Now list any positive feelings you can identify that describe how you feel about your body. Here are some examples:

proud	content	satisfied
happy	joyful	in awe
elated	confident	elegant
expectant	positive	pleased
humble	fulfilled	gratified
magnificent	comfortable	delighted
relaxed	undisturbed	whole
decent	beautiful	gorgeous
self-assured		

❧ Did you have more negative or more positive feelings?

❧ Read back over the positive feelings list. Are those feelings you want to have about your body?

❧ In chapter one you did a chronological survey of memories you have about your body. Refer to that exercise and list beside each memory any feelings you attach to that memory. You can use the feelings listed above or any other feelings that come to mind.

❧ Do you see any correlation between how you feel about your body today and how you have felt about your body throughout your life?

Often when you have a negative body image, it is caused by feelings from the past as well as the present. Negative feelings can haunt you for years unless you learn to speak the truth to them and dispel their negative influence. When my children used to be awakened by nightmares in the middle of the night, I would ask them to tell me what they had dreamed. They didn't want to tell me because their dreams frightened them so much—they just wanted to sleep in my bed and forget their awful dreams. I wanted them to tell me their dreams so they could be resolved. I would explain that their nightmares were more likely to go away if they described them.

In the same way, it's healing for women with negative body images and bad feelings from the past to talk about their negative feelings. The negative experiences and feelings deceive you into believing lies about yourself. The process of sharing those negative feelings and experiences with someone else is a first step in resolving them.

Marybeth had hated her body since she was four years old when her stepfather began molesting her. She remembered feeling dirty, ugly, and like she just wanted to disappear. These are the same feelings she had when she was asked to be a model for the fashion show. Throughout her life, she carried those negative feelings, never enjoying sex because she was so self-conscious about her body, and feeling driven to wear the latest fashions so she could attempt to cover her perceived ugliness.

In order for Marybeth to heal the negative feelings she carried, she needed to deal with her sexual abuse. She needed to feel legitimate anger at her stepfather rather than at herself, and she needed to forgive him to experience freedom in her emotions.

Forgiveness Is the Antidote to Negative Feelings Left by Others

Every woman reading this book has been hurt in some way by another person. Most of you can think of a specific instance when a person's words or actions left you despising your body. God's direction for healing from those negative feelings is through forgiveness, not through having the perfect body. Whether it's your mother who embarrassed you about your weight, your husband who rejected you, your brother who teased you incessantly, or a stranger who raped you, you will not be free of negative emotions unless you let God heal you through forgiveness.

If the person who has hurt you the most is dead, unwilling to talk to you about what happened, or a stranger, you are not prohibited from working through the process of forgiveness. Jesus died for the sins of every single person who has ever been born, yet not every single person who has ever been born will be reconciled to Jesus. We are only reconciled with Jesus and fully receive His forgiveness when we admit our sin and accept His free gift of salvation.

It is the same with our human relationships. I encourage you to work through the stages of forgiveness with any person listed in your chronological survey who has hurt you. If you need help, ask your pastor or someone at your church to encourage you through this process. You won't be sorry!

Good Feelings Are Good!

Balance is the key to positive feelings about your body. Is it okay for a woman to feel magnificent, delighted, beautiful, gorgeous, or elegant? You may wonder if you are a bad Christian if you feel that way about yourself. Personally, I would have loved to hear Marjorie say she felt beautiful, delighted, gorgeous, and elegant (plus the rest of the positive list above), even while she was 60 pounds overweight. I knew it was possible for her to feel that way. I also knew that if she felt that way, she would take better care of the body she would feel so blessed to enjoy. When her thoughts and feelings got in balance, her behaviors would follow. She might need some help from a dietitian or friend, but her desire to lose weight would develop out of her belief in and confidence about the value of her body.

I asked Marjorie to say loudly, "I'm drop-dead gorgeous to God," three times. She rolled her eyes and looked at me as if I were crazy, but she obediently complied. Each time I encouraged her to say it a little louder. By the end, she was laughing and said, "That actually made me feel better." It was as if a cloud had been lifted. After being encouraged to face how God wants her to feel about her body, the lock on her stuffed feelings of shame, betrayal, and hurt sprang open.

Step Two: Identify the ways your negative feelings are harming you. Once Marjorie felt her negative feelings, she caught up to Jana who was completely obsessed by negative feelings. Both were asked to spell out just what their negative feelings were costing them.

Marjorie made a list of the effects her negative feelings had on her own life. She recognized how she had become prejudiced against skinny people and disliked them without even knowing them. She also took note of the poor eating habits she had established and encouraged in her children. Her "I don't care" attitude had been hurtful not just to her personally, but also to others. She made the connection to her addictions to television, food, and shopping. She saw them as a distraction or escape to make her feel better.

Jana's list wasn't so hard to do. She didn't discover anything new when she wrote. She was very aware of the prison she lived in every day. She listed the parties she had begun to dress for and then skipped because her stomach stuck out too far. She thought of all the young girls in her dance class that she could have built relationships with and mentored, except that she had been too busy obsessing about her body to make a connection with them. She knew she would have more confidence as a ballerina if she could be more focused and less self-conscious about her body. Although she was acceptable as a dancer, she realized that her negative feelings were holding her back.

✿ How are your feelings about your body hurting you?

Step Three: Decide to believe the truth. Marjorie and Jana both came to the same conclusion after surveying their feelings about their bodies. They both decided they were wasting time and so much of their lives by either obsessing over or ignoring their feelings. This became the impetus to put the truths they had been learning to work for them. Each of them wrote out scriptures that reminded them how God wanted them to think about their bodies. Beside each scripture they wrote the truth about how God sees them and their bodies. Every time Marjorie was tempted to sit down and watch television, she read through the cards. Jana kept her cards in her bag and went over them during her breaks. She also recorded them on a tape to listen to in her car. Both were amazed at how different they felt after doing this for only one day.

Marjorie couldn't believe how often she felt bad about herself. She hadn't been aware of how strong her negative feelings were. It surprised her to find out that many of her decisions to watch television, eat, and shop were made in an effort to stuff down her feelings. The hardest area to resist was food. Food had a strong hold on her, and it was easy to indulge while she was home alone. She ended up putting stop signs on her refrigerator and the cabinet where the cookies were kept. A few times she ate the cookies anyway. She had a heart-to-heart talk with herself, facing up to the real reason she wanted those cookies so much. Identifying her feelings forced her to think through her emptiness.

I wonder how I can be so organized, so disciplined, so in control of most of my life, yet fail so miserably when it comes to my weight.

Marjorie discovered that emptiness was an emotion she most often filled up with food. As Marjorie thought about the empty feelings she had, she discovered some of the lies she had believed about herself. She felt empty as a stay-at-home mom. She felt angry that she did not have as much money as the two-income families in her neighborhood. She criticized herself for not being able to afford to take the family out to dinner like everyone who lived around her. Her whole neighborhood emptied out during the workweek. She was left alone with her dog Georgie, and all she had to do was watch television and eat, in between doing the chores of running a household. When Marjorie started tuning in to her feelings, she discovered that she didn't believe she was of much value to others since she stayed at home with her children and didn't get a paycheck. God's Word tells her that her worth is much more than rubies (Proverbs 31:10). She decided to start listening to God and cherish the moments she could enjoy with her children.

Jana's thinking needed a major overhaul. She recognized the immensity of the work ahead. She had drilled into her head so many lies about herself that she couldn't expect instant success. She needed to harness all the discipline she had used to shape herself into a prima ballerina. She knew that if she didn't do something, she would lose everything she had worked so tirelessly to build. Jana found an accountability partner. This was a woman who knew nothing about dancing in public, but everything about dancing with God. She knew how to let God have control of her mind so she could live in the truth.

Jana also kept up with her discipline of listening to the tape she'd made and reading over those truths during her breaks. She would journal each night about her negative and positive feelings about her body. After six months, she took an evening to read through her journal. What she discovered encouraged and surprised her. She could see how her accounts of negative feelings toward her body were getting shorter and those of her positive feelings were getting longer. This was a big breakthrough for Jana.

Step Four: Enjoy how your body feels. Most women are so hung up on how their bodies look, they miss out on how their bodies feel. God designed our bodies to give us pleasure. You need to replace some of your negative body feelings—based on shame, anger, and disgust about how you look—with positive pleasures from how your body senses the world around you.

Stop right now and softly rub your hands together. How does that feel? Is it soft and warm? Do you know that you have more nerve endings in your fingertips? Now rub your hands over your forearm. How does that feel? It is a different sensation because you don't have as many nerve endings on your forearm.

You are probably familiar with the saying, "Stop and smell the roses." Too many women don't stop and smell the roses—recognizing the wonder of their bodies. Sometimes it takes being confronted with a potentially fatal disease for a woman to begin to appreciate her body. Your body is an amazing combination of traits conceived by an extremely creative God. We miss out on enjoying and appreciating our bodies when we fail to recognize that fact.

Both Jana and Marjorie were challenged to get more in touch with their body sensations every day. Each was told to literally stop and smell the roses, engaging her sense of smell to bring positive feelings about her body.

You too need to tune in to the world around you through your body's amazing senses. Make special efforts to experience your sense of touch. Touch children, hug your friends, get a massage, shake hands, all the time being conscious of your body's enjoyment of pleasure. Cultivate your senses of smell, taste, touch, sight, and hearing.

When you are on a binge-eating craze, you don't taste, see, or smell your food. Get some chocolate ice cream (or your favorite flavor). Eat it slowly. Feel the coolness, the smooth texture. Enjoy the smell and don't miss the taste of your ice cream cone. When you eat this way, you will eat more slowly and with more satisfaction. You won't be eating to stuff your feelings but to enjoy your feelings. Praise God for the wonder of ice cream as you eat.

Being aware of your body's sensations is part of your connection to other people. When we meet new people, we often shake hands. We hug relatives we haven't seen in a while. Giving a hug is a sign of the deeper connection that we make with them.

Try one of the following activities to increase your awareness of your physical feelings:

1. Take time to enjoy a beautiful sunrise or sunset. Let your eyes enjoy the vision of this colorful masterpiece.

2. Make a special effort to touch objects and appropriately touch people in a 24-hour period. As you sit down at your desk, run your hand across the smooth wood. Touch flowers and pets, give more hugs, take time to feel the wonder of your world.

3. Discipline yourself to slowly chew every bite you put into your mouth. Think of a special food that you enjoy. Take a certain amount of time to eat it, savoring the taste.

4. Listen to the sounds of nature in a park near your house. Tune in to the birds chirping, the wind blowing, the water running. Try to identify as many different sounds as you can.

5. Celebrate your sense of smell. Go to a flower garden and take in the scent of each bloom.

Step Five: Eliminate body shame and sexual shame. Deep beneath Jana's shame about her body was a secret she kept carefully hidden. She never wanted to admit to herself or anyone else what happened to her the summer she was 15 and visiting her father at his home several states away. Her father worked during the day and she was left to hang out with the neighborhood kids whom she had never met before. They were a little faster than the crowd she hung out with at home. She turned down several invitations to parties at night, but she felt safe to play pool or hang out at the home of a neighbor, Stacy. One day, near the end of the summer, Tony came to the house. Jana was instantly attracted to this good-looking guy. After a game of pool, they sat down together on the couch in Stacy's basement.

At age 54, I pretty much have accepted what I have,
although I could stand to lose five pounds.

Jana didn't notice it at the time, but as if on cue, all the other kids disappeared from the basement. She was alone with Tony. He continued flirting with her. She felt fine with this, but when he pushed her to fool around more, she began to feel uncomfortable. Tony was very good at getting what he wanted, and without totally realizing what was happening, Jana became a victim of date rape in a few short minutes.

After he was finished, Tony went over to the pool table and invited her to play a game. When she was able to pull herself together, she ran to her father's house without looking at anyone. There was no one home, so she ran to the bathroom and showered for an hour. She was leaving in two days, and she asked her father to let her spend the last two nights at her grandma's house. She wanted to call her mom, but she knew how much it made her dad mad when she called her mom on his visitations. By the time she got home, she didn't even tell her mom. She found her best escape in pretending she had never laid eyes on Tony. On a good day, she couldn't even remember his name, even when she tried.

There are so many women like Jana and Marybeth whose negative feelings about their bodies are intertwined with unwanted sexual experiences, or shameful sexual activities in which they participated. It is necessary for women to be healed from their sexual shame in order to be at peace with their bodies. There are a great number of women with eating disorders who have been sexually abused. A strong correlation exists between mistreating your body with food, bingeing, purging, and so on, and having an emotional vault deep inside filled with sexual shame.

Like Marybeth, you may have negative feelings about your body as the result of sexual abuse. If so, you need to heal from that wound through forgiveness; otherwise you remain a victim. If your negative feelings about your body are associated with sexual sin from the past, you need to receive God's cleansing through forgiveness.

> If we confess our sins, he is faithful and just and will forgive us our sins and purify us from all unrighteousness (1 John 1:9).

❧ What is our part in being forgiven for past and present sins?

❧ What does God do when we confess?

Part of learning to let go of negative feelings about your body is receiving God's forgiveness. If you are trapped in the pit of shame and disgrace because of sexual experiences you've had, God invites you to be cleansed. I love the way God describes what actually happens when He forgives us. He grants us a clean slate. He literally cleanses us from

the stain of sin. We are made new through His cleansing blood! You
don't have to feel defiled by sexual shame and sin. You can be clean.

Step Six: Feel confident in your own body. The payoff to all that
hard work is feeling confident in the body you live in. So what if your
tummy is a little round? You can work out three times a week. You can
lift and bend and perform all the movements necessary to do your
laundry, walk the dog, or fly a kite. Your body is amazing! When you
know that, you'll feel different. You'll still have a round tummy, but
you'll have a different response to it. It won't make you feel disgusted,
ashamed, or unworthy. It is a part of being human. It is a fact of life.

Your feelings will change when you get the right thoughts in your
mind. The choice is yours. You can feel confident or contemptible.
Your feelings are based on what you think. Your focus changes from
how you want to look to how you want to *feel* about how you look.
Feeling good inside your body is evidence of a healthy body image.

Recently, I attended a mother-son campout. It was a wonderful
weekend. My friend Tammy, who invited me, had told me about the
ropes course the moms would be asked to do. We were supposed to
climb up a telephone pole, walk across another telephone pole until
we came to a flimsy wire that we had to walk over, and finally jump
off a platform and down a zipline. She told me it wasn't mandatory,
but that my son would be so proud of me for trying. As I stood in line,
my feet and the palms of my hands literally filled with sweat at the
prospect of such a feat. (Did I mention that we wore harnesses
attached to ropes that would catch us if we fell?)

I put on my helmet and climbed up the pole. As I stood facing the
opposite direction, I thought: *I could jump right now and let the line
catch me.* I didn't want to move forward and felt terrified of walking
out on that very high and very narrow pole. Rather than give in to my
feelings, I prayed and asked God to help me get across. I put my trust
in Him, not in my own ability. My feelings of utter terror turned into
feelings of peace, and I calmly walked across the pole.

High-climbing stunts may not be for you. But the high-flying experience of confidence in the body you live in is what God has in store. You can become free of your despair. You can live in confidence. You can soar emotionally. Keep your thoughts on God's Word. Accept God's values; receive God's help. Your whole emotional well-being can change as a result.

Discussion Questions

1. How can your feelings crush your spirit?

2. Why do some women stuff their feelings?

3. Why do other women obsess over their feelings?

4. Why is what we believe important to changing our feelings?

5. Share an example of how you have experienced inner healing through forgiveness.

6. What are some of the favorite sensations you can enjoy with your body?

CHAPTER EIGHT

Anchored in God's Word

Misty got pregnant the first time she had sex—the night of her senior prom. Throughout the summer that followed, she lived in denial that she could possibly be pregnant. Before she went to college, at her annual physical, she finally faced the facts. Her church and parents were overwhelmingly supportive. Surrounded by God's grace, Misty made a difficult but loving decision to allow her baby daughter to be adopted by a Christian couple. There was joy and heartache for all involved. Afterward, the stretch marks on her abdomen were a poignant reminder she faced each day. When she looked at them, she condemned herself for being so stupid and getting pregnant and managing to make such a mess of her life.

Those stretch marks were a repulsive reminder of the high cost of sin, and they threatened to send Misty into despair. "What kind of good Christian man could ever love a woman who's done what I've done and who looks like this?" is the kind of question she asked in her depression. It took a whole lot of faith to confront the disparaging remarks that erupted in her head. Misty needed to be built back up by believing God's Word and becoming anchored in His love for her.

Misty's hopes for human love and romance aren't over because she has a few stretch marks. In fact, they may help steer her to the right man after all. The kind of man she needs is the kind of man who will love her unconditionally, the way God does. As Misty believes God's Word, she'll be ready to discover God's man for her.

God's Word and Our Bodies

We have already looked at many scriptures that apply to body image. A few will be repeated here; they bear repeating. Just like Misty, you need to get your head full of God's Word to overcome your negative body image. Let's summarize some of the principles we can draw from Scripture about how God sees our bodies.

1. God knows humans are tempted to overemphasize how a person looks in evaluating his or her character. For example, let's revisit 1 Samuel, in which Samuel was instructed to look for a new king among Jesse's sons.

> But the Lord said to Samuel, "Do not consider his appearance or his height, for I have rejected him. The Lord does not look at the things man looks at. Man looks at the outward appearance, but the Lord looks at the heart" (1 Samuel 16:7).

�烋 When Samuel was looking for the man God intended to be king over Israel, what did God tell him?

Samuel was a great prophet of God. His very conception was established in prayer. (His mother Hannah was barren and went to the temple to pray for a child. See 1 Samuel 1 for the story.) His entire life was dedicated to God. He remained forever faithful to God throughout his life, in spite of the poor examples of leadership provided by the priest Eli and his sons, under whom he served. Samuel knew the Word of God and obeyed it painstakingly. When God determined that Saul should no longer be the king of Israel and decided to have Samuel anoint a new king, He gave the warning you just read. He told Samuel not to be surprised if the king God chose didn't look like much of a king.

I lost my toe in a biking accident when I was 10. Since then, I've become a magician in disguising this hideous part of me.

If a great prophet of God like Samuel can be misled by appearances, no wonder the same thing happens to you and me. We need to heed the same warning about appearances that God gave Samuel. We need to be more concerned about how beautiful our hearts are than our looks.

2. God does not place the emphasis on outward appearance that humans do. Again, let's consider Jesus' appearance.

> He grew up before him like a tender shoot, and like a root out of dry ground. He had no beauty or majesty to attract us to him, nothing in his appearance that we should desire him (Isaiah 53:2).

🌿 How would you design your body if you were creating one for yourself?

If you or I could decide how we were to look, we would probably throw in a lot of extra-beautiful characteristics. God purposefully chose to leave them out of Jesus' human body when He became man.

God will not be holding beauty pageants in heaven. He created the differences in physical characteristics that in combination create true beauty. God certainly enjoys beauty, but one person's beauty does not diminish someone else in God's view.

Misty wouldn't have thought stretch marks could be beauty marks. But Linda, her baby's adoptive mother, would have gladly endured 10 times as many stretch marks just to be a mother. Misty began to realize that those stretch marks are beauty marks to God. She did a beautiful and loving thing by not aborting her daughter and by allowing her to be raised by loving parents.

3. God knows women are particularly interested in making themselves look nice. Let's look at 1 Peter 3:3–4.

> ³Your beauty should not come from outward adornment, such as braided hair and the wearing of gold jewelry and fine clothes. ⁴Instead, it should be that of your inner self, the unfading beauty of a gentle and quiet spirit, which is of great worth in God's sight.

❧ What kind of adorning does God think is beautiful in women?

Women are adorners. There is something inside most of us that drives us to make ourselves look our best. God doesn't condemn that. He does condemn getting overly caught up in outward beauty, though. He knows that is important to us, but He wants so much more for us. God encourages women not to ignore true beauty by merely focusing on externals. He longs for us to cultivate the internal qualities of a gentle and quiet spirit.

To develop our internal qualities, it's important to spend time with God. We need to rely on the Holy Spirit to fill us with love, joy, peace, patience, kindness, goodness, faithfulness, gentleness, and self-control (Galatians 5:22–23). A gentle and quiet spirit is the result of placing your full trust in God—not in your looks, talents, or abilities.

4. What we think we look like on the outside depends on how we feel about ourselves in general. At first, all the bride of Solomon could think about was her skin, which she thought was ugly. But later, even though her skin hadn't changed, she liked herself and felt she was beautiful. In Song of Songs 1:6 she says, "Do not stare at me because I am swarthy, for the sun has burned me"(NASB). One chapter later she says, "I am the rose of Sharon, the lily of the valleys" (Song of Songs 2:1, NASB).

🌿 What changed about the bride of Solomon that made her like herself?

We've already discovered that body image is not based on what we look like on the outside, but on what we think about how we look. The bride of Solomon is a true example of this. Her skin color didn't change, but her feelings about her physical being did. The change occurred in her head—what she thought about how she looked.

5. It's fine to wear nice clothes and be well groomed as long as you keep this in balance with other qualities. Consider the Proverbs 31 woman.

> She makes coverings for her bed; she is clothed in fine
> linen and purple (Proverbs 31:22).

🌿 Is it okay for Christian women to wear fine clothing?

This outstanding woman's clothing was of a fine quality, but her clothes are mentioned only briefly among her many wonderful characteristics: caring for the needs of the household, working with her hands, helping the poor, and others.

The list of this woman's qualities has challenged women through the years. There appears to be simply nothing that she couldn't do. Some say that it was all the servants in her household that helped her get so much done. In any case, she was a very dutiful, productive woman. It is liberating in a way to think about her clothes of fine linen.

It is not bad or sinful for women to like attractive clothes. God does not forbid us to decorate our homes in beauty and comfort. It is only when you let pursuing beauty get out of hand that it becomes a problem. It is natural to want to look the best you can. But you can look as nice when you buy your clothes at a discount store as you do when you buy them at the finest clothing store around. The important thing isn't the label—it's the balance you find in your life.

6. You can be outwardly beautiful and still be unattractive to others. Proverbs has much to say about this subject.

> Like a gold ring in a pig's snout is a beautiful woman who shows no discretion (Proverbs 11:22).
> Charm is deceptive, and beauty is fleeting; but a woman who fears the Lord is to be praised (Proverbs 31:30).

✤ How is it possible to be outwardly beautiful, but not attractive?

✤ What is necessary to be attractive?

It's not just how you look on the outside that makes you beautiful. Beauty is a combination of many characteristics. First Corinthians 13, the great love chapter, is a wonderful description of what God would consider truly beautiful. Let it remind you of someone in your life whose beauty is defined not by her physical characteristics but by her actions.

7. God decided that our bodies are the best temple for Him to dwell in.

> What agreement is there between the temple of God and idols? For we are the temple of the living God (2 Corinthians 6:16).

✺ What does it mean to you that your body is the temple of God? (If you are a Christian, the Holy Spirit lives inside of you.)

King Solomon built the first permanent physical temple for God to dwell within. Second Chronicles 2–7 details the extravagant preparations that went into building this temple. It had been King David's desire to build it, but God denied him that privilege because he had shed innocent blood. David instilled the desire to build the temple into his son Solomon.

I'm ashamed of how my obesity has caused so many other problems.
My back and knees can't bear the weight. I've stopped having periods.
I just feel like a big, ugly mess.

Building the temple was one of the first tasks Solomon undertook for the nation of Israel. It was an elaborate endeavor. When it was all done, the ark of the covenant was ceremonially placed in the Holy of Holies, its proper abode. Yet one thing remained unfinished: God's presence wasn't there. Solomon prayed for God's presence (see chapter six) and when Solomon finished praying, "fire came down from heaven and consumed the burnt offering and the sacrifices, and the glory of the Lord filled the temple" (2 Chronicles 7:1).

Later God appeared to Solomon and told him, "I have heard your prayer and have chosen this place for myself as a temple for sacrifices" (2 Chronicles 7:12).

It struck me one day when I was reading this passage that Solomon could have gone to all that work for nothing. The temple wouldn't have been the temple of God if God had not chosen to dwell there. God could have said "no," and all of Solomon's work would have been in vain.

That made it even more significant to me that God now chooses to dwell in our earthly bodies. Our human flesh-and-blood bodies are His choice for where He wants to live. Isn't that unbelievable? My body, with all of its flaws, is where God chooses to abide. He wants to live in me—just the way I look now, not when I lose a few pounds. He created me, and He desires to dwell in me!

8. God made our bodies, and that alone makes them wonderful.

> I praise you because I am fearfully and wonderfully
> made; your works are wonderful, I know that full well
> (Psalm 139:14).

❧ Is the work of your body wonderful?

The number one reason to honor the body God gave you is because He made you. King David, the author of this psalm, understood this in a unique way.

Occasionally I catch the Oprah Winfrey program while I am getting dinner ready. Over the years I have been amazed by her poor body image. She is constantly putting herself down for not being skinny. So I was thrilled for her the day the program about new medical tests aired. It was about an X-ray machine used to detect medical problems before symptoms occur. The machine scans the body from several different perspectives.

I am humiliated by my stretch marks.

After having the test and viewing the inside of her own body, Oprah experienced a dramatic shift. She said, "I've changed my whole paradigm, because you know I've been on every diet in America. Some

I invented, some I borrowed from other people, but for the first time after doing this test, I decided I'm no longer going to eat or exercise for my hips. I'm doing it for my heart."[1] During the program, she mentioned several times that she loved her heart, and that she hadn't eaten a potato chip since she saw the scan of her heart. Oprah had a King David experience. She got a better glimpse into her body and the mystery it is, and it changed her life.

9. God wants to make all things new in your life. Consider 2 Corinthians 5:17.

> Therefore, if anyone is in Christ, he is a new creation; the
> old has gone, the new has come!

🌿 What does God want to do in your life?

🌿 How has God made your body image new?

As strange as it sounds, some women have a hard time enjoying new feelings about their bodies. When you have hated parts of your body for many years, it's hard to feel like you are still you without the hate. It's like getting a different haircut. At first you look in the mirror and don't recognize the reflection. It takes a couple of days to integrate the new haircut into who you think you are. It's the same way when your body image begins to change. There will be an adjustment period.

Testing in the Wilderness

I can almost guarantee that your new body image freedom will be tested. It will be tested each time you watch a commercial on TV promoting the latest wrinkle remover. It will be tested when you look at your stomach sticking out or notice your legs when you try on shorts in the dressing room.

Jesus was tested in the wilderness. Just after He was baptized in the Jordan, He heard a voice out of heaven saying, "This is my Son, whom I love; with him I am well pleased" (Matthew 3:17). Then He was led by the Spirit to the wilderness to be tested (Matthew 4:1–11). This may confuse some. You might wonder, "Why would God test me?" God tests you to build your confidence and your effectiveness. You could easily close this book and go back to thinking about your body the same way as you always have. God tests you to help you grow.

Smith and Graybeal say, "How could God instigate Jesus' temptation? The word translated 'to be tempted' actually means 'to be tested.' There is a subtle but important difference. God tests; the devil tempts. God does not want Jesus to fail; the devil does."[2] It is very important for you to understand that each time you are tempted to hate your body and sink back into self-loathing, it is an opportunity to rely on God for strength and confidence.

Prayer prepares you to stand strong in the temptations and testing that will definitely come into your life.

> [36]Then Jesus went with his disciples to a place called Gethsemane, and he said to them, "Sit here while I go over there and pray." [37]He took Peter and the two sons of Zebedee along with him, and he began to be sorrowful and troubled. [38]Then he said to them, "My soul is overwhelmed with sorrow to the point of death. Stay here and keep watch with me." [39]Going a little farther, he fell with his face to the ground and prayed, "My Father, if it is possible, may this cup be taken from me. Yet not as I will, but as you will." [40]Then he returned to his disciples and found them sleeping. "Could you men not keep watch with me for one hour?" he asked Peter. [41]"Watch and pray so that you will not fall into temptation. The spirit is willing, but the body is weak" (Matthew 26:36–41).

How did prayer affect Jesus' ability to fulfill God's plan for Him?

❧ What did Jesus correct the disciples about?

This time of prayer became a critical characteristic of Jesus' journey to the cross. Jesus came to this earth as a baby to reconcile the hostilities between God and man. He had no other purpose but to do the will of the Father. He demonstrated this over and over by the choices He made each day. When Jesus prayed for the cup to be taken from Him, He demonstrated His complete reliance on God to fulfill His mission. Jesus trusted God's answer to His prayer, that dying on the cross was the only way. He walked that steady path to the cross. Prayer gave Him the strength to go forward with God's plan.

I hate my big nose.

Jesus encouraged the disciples to pray for themselves so they wouldn't fall into temptation. You need to pray for yourself too. Prayer was the key to Jesus' victory over sin, and it is the key to your victory over body hate.

❧ Write a prayer to God, asking for His help in overcoming your body hate. Here's an example:

Dear God:

    I want to submit my body, mind, and soul to You. I need Your help to resist Satan as he easily tempts me to criticize my body and feel that I am not good enough. I accept Your love for me. I know that You do not look at my body the way the world does. I know that my body is fearfully and wonderfully made. I yield myself to You and ask that You give me power to resist the devil just as You did for Jesus.

Now that you have set the groundwork by prayer, you are launched on your journey to freedom.

Victory Is Possible

Working on your body image depends on changing the way you think more than on changing your body. Working on your body image will result in changes in your body, mind, and soul. God created you with a mysterious connection between the three. As you change your thinking, your body benefits by discovering more energy. Your soul is tended as you discover God's truth about yourself.

You see, when you are thinking about Truth (God's Word); taking care of your body through proper rest, eating, and exercise cycles; and tending to your spiritual self, then all three parts of you—body, mind, and soul—function in balance. When you stop making your body the scapegoat for all the pain and hurt you have suffered, equilibrium and balance will enter your life.

> Remember that chronological survey you completed in chapter one? Are you ready to tear it out of your journal and throw those memories and experiences away? If so, do that as a sign of the victory God has given you.

It's time to make practical changes in your mind, will, and emotions. It's time to break the chains of body hate. Misty's stretch marks have faded a bit; the evidence of being anchored in God's Word is more apparent in her life. Presently, she is dating a seminary student who treats her the way God wants her to be treated. Because she has focused on God's Word as truth, she no longer sees her stretch marks as an obstacle to love.

Discussion Questions

1. How can you fight your human tendency to look on the outside rather than at the heart?

2. How does God's Word help us get the right perspective on our bodies?

3. How can you balance looking nice with living for God, as the Proverbs 31 woman did?

4. What does it mean to you that your body is God's temple?

5. Describe a time when you discovered a new appreciation for your body.

6. What are the benefits of having a positive view of your body?

CHAPTER NINE

Healthier Ever After

This study isn't meant to be an 11-week reprieve from self-loathing. My hope is that you will break free from the trap of body hate and genuinely enjoy the wonder of your body for the rest of your life. I long for you to accept the body you live in and have an accurate grasp of its significance toward your existence on earth. It's not as if there is a perfect cure for the disease of body hate. From time to time you may still wish for a flatter stomach, thinner thighs, or a remedy for whatever it is that bothers you most. But you can live free of self-loathing by learning how to believe the truth about who you are. God longs for us to be confident women focused on living in and enjoying our bodies, not being enslaved to them.

> ³Your beauty should not come from outward adornment, such as braided hair and the wearing of gold jewelry and fine clothes. ⁴Instead, it should be that of your inner self, the unfading beauty of a gentle and quiet spirit, which is of great worth in God's sight. ⁵For this is the way the holy women of the past who put their hope in God used to make themselves beautiful (1 Peter 3:3–5).

What does beauty not come from?

What is true beauty—beauty that never fades?

My husband's grandfather often told his wife that she was as beautiful as the day he first laid eyes on her. Brian and I stayed with his grandmother the night of his grandfather's funeral. We sat on the bed with her as she reflected on the day he died at home in her arms. She said, "That morning he told me that I looked as beautiful as the day he first met me when I was 16." Indeed, she was ultimate beauty to him—even with her wrinkles, sparse hair, and thick glasses. Her beauty hadn't faded with the passage of time, but had grown stronger. Her beauty sprang from the loving and caring relationship she shared with him. That relationship had grown even more precious with time.

It didn't take me long to figure out that I was a freak.
I was born with deformed fingers, and kids were cruel!
I don't even try to imagine what it might be like to be pretty.
I know I will never be seen that way, so I focus on being smart.

That's the same way God sees us according to this scripture. Our beauty is revealed even in the body flaws we each carry. Our beauty is in a gentle and quiet spirit. When you read the words gentle and quiet, you might think of a meek and timid person. But you can be loud and outgoing and still be gentle and quiet in your spirit. A gentle and quiet spirit is exhibited as you place your complete trust in God. When a woman stops struggling to be what everyone else thinks she should be, and instead lets herself enjoy what God thinks she should be, she portrays a gentle and quiet spirit. A woman with a gentle and quiet spirit feels assured of her beauty to God.

Breaking the Chains

Marybeth was challenged to let go of her controlling behaviors in regard to her body. She's the one who refused to be a model for the women's ministry fashion show. After working through her grief and anger and forgiving her stepfather for sexually abusing her, Marybeth needed to face her own sins. One of them was the way she looked at her body. Even though she looked the best she could, she never felt satisfied and confident in her own skin.

She practiced the mind makeover for weeks and weeks, and decided the best way to show she was accepting God's love for her was to attend the women's retreat without wearing makeup the whole morning. She made this decision privately; it was just between herself and God. This is what she wrote about her experience:

> God,
> I can't believe how completely You have set me free. Me, the one who wouldn't even get in front of women with all my makeup on went, not just the morning, but the whole day without makeup. You know, no one even noticed. I thought for sure everyone would ask me if I was sick or something, but not one person said a thing. Oh God, forgive me for the years I have wasted hating my body and trying to avoid rejection about how I look. I so over-personalized everything. No one looks at me the way I thought they did. No one was ever as cruel to me about my looks as I was to myself. Thank You for this insight and victory this weekend. It is such a blessing to be loved by a God as wonderful as You. Help me share this with my daughter, Kathy. Sometimes I recognize that she does so many of the same things I used to do.

Paul wrote to the church at Philippi (Philippians 1:6) that he was confident of their spiritual growth. I am confident that as long as you let the truth of God's Word enter fully into your life, you too will become more and more confident in your body. You will grasp the reality of true beauty. You will understand that beauty is about character, not whether your arms wiggle in the wind.

Body Hate Relapse Plan

It takes work to make changes in your thought patterns and feelings. You can't just expect that since you've read all these scriptures and almost finished this book that you will never need to address this area of your life again. It is very likely that you will struggle to keep negative body stress at a minimum, but the key to succeeding is to be prepared. Here are some suggestions to help you stay on track:

1. Accept that you are not perfect. If you make it your goal to never have a negative thought or feeling about your body again, you are setting yourself up for failure. Be realistic in your expectations.

In general, I feel okay. But if I stop and think about it,
I know I could tone up everywhere.

----

2. Take inventory of your mind. What you keep in your mind is the most important factor in maintaining a healthy body image. You need to take every thought captive in order to attain the emotional, psychological, and spiritual peace you are seeking.

3. Get enough rest for your body. So many women underestimate their need for rest. They set themselves up for failure because they aren't concerned with how tired they are. Rest is vital to emotional, spiritual, and physical wellness. You may have to decide to let go of certain areas of your life in order to care for your body adequately. Americans are not good at resting. Most push themselves to work, play, and do, so they cannot fit enough rest into a 24-hour day. Often, overeating is related to fatigue. When your body feels sluggish and out of sorts, instead of a nap, you grab a candy bar for energy. If you get enough rest, you will be better able to attend to the issues that you face each day.

4. Recognize negative feelings and deal with them daily. We've already stated that the temptation to belittle yourself will be a reality to deal with. Your feelings will sound the alarm; the first time you become aware of self-disgust, take notice. Don't let that negative feeling slide, or it will build up to an endless number of negative feelings and thoughts. Stop yourself right then and there. Examine the feeling, tell God about the feeling, journal about it, and wrestle with the truth about it.

5. Enlist an accountability partner/prayer partner. Do you remember how much Jesus encouraged His disciples to pray to avoid temptation? Prayer is a powerful and effective tool. God promises that when two or more are gathered in His name He is there with them (Matthew 18:20). Take advantage of this important advice. Find a prayer partner whom you can call at a particularly bad time. You don't have to pray only about body image; you can pray about other issues as well.

6. Reread the book and complete the exercises. It is very important for you to reread books that have had a particular impact on you. You may think you have received everything a book has to offer after you've read it once. But later you may be at a different place and need to think through some of those issues again. You may need extra encouragement to let the truth sink into your total being.

7. Don't judge how others look. A sure way to maintain the newer, healthier you is to examine how you look at and talk about others' bodies. When you are less critical of others, you will be less critical of yourself. Think something positive about the actress on television who has aged since you saw her last. Think about how great it is that the woman in the wheelchair is able to get around the grocery store the way she can. Try to see people beyond what is on the outside. Think about people the way God thinks of them: He looks at their hearts.

8. Don't receive criticism about how you look from others. Many women are in relationships with husbands, mothers, boyfriends, children, coworkers, bosses, and others who criticize their appearance. When you aren't the only one criticizing yourself, it is more difficult to maintain a healthy body image. If you are in this situation, my heart goes out to you because you are in a painful relationship. You need the prayers and support of your group to help you. It's easy for me to say, "Don't listen to those who criticize you," but it is much more difficult for you to put it into practice. Make up your mind to resist these negative words with the help of God and your study or prayer group.

When my weight started fluctuating in my thirties I started a training program for a marathon. It did wonders for my overall health and fitness, and controlled my weight as well.

9. Write yourself a letter. In counseling I often ask individuals to write a letter to themselves about a new truth they are learning. It's time to write yourself a letter explaining the truths you've learned about your body. Keep the letter and read it every time you feel negative feelings about your body.

Here's what Marybeth wrote:

> Dear Marybeth:
>   God wants you to fully accept that you are beautiful to Him. You are His creation. He made you. You are wonderfully made. Even though your stepfather hurt you

in your body and soul, it doesn't make what God made dirty or ugly. When you are feeling dirty, ugly, fat, made wrong, and inadequate, you are believing the lie Satan placed in your mind when you were four years old. You've listened to that lie for so many years, it is hard to stop it, but with the help of the Holy Spirit you can be free.

God has set you free from the lie. You can choose to live in His truth and be free to enjoy the rest of His creation, or you can choose to sink back into the mire and darkness of your miserable thinking. The choice is yours! I know you will make the right one.

I'm proud of how you look, body flaws and all!

Marybeth

❧ Take some time now to write a letter in your journal.

10. Recognize the symptoms of relapse. Here is a checklist that will help you recognize the symptoms of relapse before they go too far. Check any questions that are true of you.

_____ Am I getting inadequate rest for my body?

_____ Am I projecting my bad feelings about my body onto others? (I know my friend noticed that I gained 10 pounds, but she is too nice to mention it.)

_____ Am I impatient about the physical results of eating better and exercising?

_____ Am I irritable with others?

_____ Am I feeling depressed about my body?

_____ Am I suffering from self-pity? (Why do my thighs have to be shaped this way?)

_____ Do I think I've got my self-loathing conquered and believe I can handle anything?

_____ Do I agree with others who make self-loathing statements?

_____ Am I being too hard on myself in other areas now, in place of how I used to self-criticize my body?

_____ Am I ungrateful for the wonder of my body, its senses, complicated systems, etc.?

_____ Do I think I've come too far now to fall back again?

If you checked even one statement, you have a problem with relapse. Two or more checks mean that you are dangerously close to relapse.

Tips for Looking Your Best

Esther spent an entire year in beauty treatments. It is not sinful to think about how you look and to try to look your best. But it is sinful when your appearance becomes your identity. There are two unhealthy responses women can make—one is to put too much emphasis on their appearance, and the other is to ignore how they look entirely.

I feel very insecure about my bra size.

Paying attention to looks should be important to Christian women. In fact, Paul included some instructions for women about their appearance in his letters to Timothy in which he explained the doctrines and disciplines of the church.

> [9]I also want women to dress modestly, with decency and
> propriety, not with braided hair or gold or pearls or
> expensive clothes, [10]but with good deeds, appropriate for
> women who profess to worship God (1 Timothy 2:9–10).

❧ Why does God want women to dress modestly?

God wants women to dress modestly and with decency so everything in their lives reveals their reverence for Him. If you've ever searched for a home, you know what it is like to enter the homes of strangers with your Realtor. You can tell a lot about the homeowners by the way they decorate. Workers I've had in my home have mentioned that they can tell I'm a Christian. In your home there are clues to your priorities beyond what you say and how you live. Likewise, there are clues to your relationship with God in the clothes that you wear. It is important to think about your appearance and what it reveals to the world about your devotion to God.

🌾 Describe how you think Christian women should dress.

I don't think Christian women should wear a uniform or look exactly alike. In fact, I think these beauty tips by Audrey Hepburn are very appropriate for Christian women:

> For attractive lips, Speak words of kindness.
> For lovely eyes, Seek out the good in people.
> For a slim figure, Share your food with the hungry.
> For beautiful hair, Let a child run his or her fingers
>   through it once a day.
> For poise, Walk with the knowledge you'll never walk alone.[1]

Since we are on the subject of beauty tips, I share my practical advice about outward beauty in Appendix I. If you have time, I suggest you read over that appendix right now. If not, go back to it later.

God's Role in Liking the Body I Live In

The number one reason not to berate and mistreat your body is because God is the One who created you. He loves you, and when you love someone you don't want to see her berating herself. How do you let God be the reason you love your body?

Don't feel shame about your body when it comes to your relationship with God. He doesn't look down on you because you have a desire to look nice. In fact, God wants to be your partner in your plan to care for your body. Symeon the New Theologian (A.D. 949–1022) wrote this revealing poem:

> We awaken in Christ's body
> as Christ awakens our bodies,
> and my poor hand is Christ,
> He enters my foot,
> and is infinitely me.
>
> I move my hand,
> and wonderfully
> my hand becomes Christ,
> becomes all of Him
> (for God is indivisibly
> whole, seamless in His Godhood).
>
> I move my foot, and at once
> He appears like a flash
> of lightning.
>
> Do my words
> seem blasphemous?
>
> Then open your heart to Him and let yourself receive
> the one who is opening
> to you so deeply.
>
> For if we genuinely love Him,
> we wake up inside
> Christ's body where all our body, all over,
> every most hidden part of it,
> is realized in joy as Him,
> And He makes us, utterly, real,
> And everything that is hurt,

everything that seemed to us dark, harsh, shameful, maimed,
ugly, irreparably damaged,
is in Him transformed
and recognized as whole,
as lovely,
and radiant in His light.

We awaken as the beloved
in every last part of our body.[2]

Discussion Questions

1. What is true beauty according to 1 Peter 3:4–5?

2. What does a gentle and quiet spirit look like in a woman?

3. What steps can you take to guard against relapse?

4. Share practical tips you've found for making over your clothes, makeup, and so on.

5. What is the right perspective about food and how you eat?

6. Read the letter you wrote to yourself about who you are and the truths you've learned about your body.

CHAPTER TEN

How to Help Others Develop a Healthy Body Image

Do you know a woman or girl who never makes a negative comment about her body? Probably not. The problem of negative body image is epidemic in American culture and the developed world. Christian women who have a healthy body image can be a beacon to others by their influence in the way they talk about, treat, and honor their bodies. I've had opportunities to talk to secular audiences on this subject. Afterward, I am almost always approached by someone who asks if I am a Christian. They can see that there is something deeper than just human reason and knowledge that gives me the foundation for the information I share.

You may not teach or speak on this subject, but there are opportunities for you to get involved in making the world a safer place for girls and women. If you are a mother, your realm of influence is great. You need to be thoughtful, not only about the example you set for a healthy body image, but also regarding the words you say about your children's bodies. You can contact advertisers and boycott products that are specifically degrading to women. You also have an influence on the women in your social circles. Let's look at ways you can be challenged to be an agent of change in your world.

Like Mother, Like Daughter

Mothers have a unique connection to their daughters. Mothers need to be very intentional about the way they talk to their children (both sons and daughters) about their bodies. From the moment a baby comes home, mothers are mainly responsible for caring for their bodies. They feed them, decide when a rash is a bug bite, hives, or eczema, and determine the proper treatment. Children come to moms with aches and pains, skinned knees and sore throats. Moms show their children how to bathe and brush their teeth. Moms fix hair and pick out children's clothes.

I can't stand the way I have a little pouch
around my belly, just like my mom.

Sometimes moms get so used to this role, they fail to let their children grow up. Moms also have a tendency to think that they are so much a part of their children that it is okay to talk about their pimples, fat, and so on in a way that they would never talk to a best friend.

What Do Kids Need to Hear from Their Mothers about Their Bodies?

There are several messages that you want to get across to your children.

1. You want them to know that they are fearfully and wonderfully made (Psalm 139:14). You know the saying, "She has a face only a mother could love." Well, all children need to be sure that their parents approve of their bodies. This is hard to do if you think your child is not taking care of his or her body.

Please don't underestimate the power your words have in the self-esteem of your child. I see a common thread in the women I have treated with eating disorders. Many had parents who put them on diets and tried whatever means available to make them look perfect on the outside. This backfires in your relationship with your child, and usually becomes a block to your child's success and happiness in life.

Instead of being part of the problem, I challenge you to use your influence to impact your children positively. From the time they can talk you can teach them that they are wonderfully made. You can talk to your little ones about their scrapes and bruises. Point out how wonderful our bodies are as you watch new skin develop. Get a book about bodies to read with younger children. Talk about your own body in positive ways with your children. Children listen to everything you say. When you talk about how you look like a beached whale in your bathing suit, it has an effect on your child.

You want to be sure that you get across to your children that appearance is important, but not essential. It is not mandatory for your child to look a certain way in order to believe that his or her body is fearfully and wonderfully made. Teach your children to respect their bodies by the way they rest, exercise, and eat.

2. As your children grow you need to teach them that God knows their body flaws. You can teach your children to trust God with hurts, including pain about physical appearance. Encourage them to ask God what good could come out of their limitations.

> "O house of Israel, can I not do with you as this potter
> does?" declares the Lord. "Like clay in the hand of the potter,
> so are you in my hand, O house of Israel" (Jeremiah 18:6).

✿ How is your body like clay in the potter's hands?

✿ How have you seen God receive glory in your body flaws?

✿ How can your children be drawn closer to God because of their body flaws?

It will be difficult to teach your children how to accept their body flaws if you haven't been able to accept your own. That is why it is so beneficial for you to do this study. Do you need to accept that God knows your body flaws and desires to be close to you and comfort you about any pain these flaws have caused?

I see parents actually harm their children when they try to give them everything. Children learn from disappointment. The worst thing you can do is to try to fix all your children's body flaws in order to help them attain beauty by the world's standards. Rather, teach your children how to keep their body flaws in perspective.

3. You also need to teach your children that their bodies are the temple of God. If your child is a Christian, the Holy Spirit chooses to dwell in his or her body. This is the reason Paul said not to join with a prostitute (1 Corinthians 6:15–16). If God lives in their bodies, it must make their bodies very special. Not only should they honor God with their bodies by following God's sexual standards, but also honor their bodies by not criticizing and rejecting their own flesh and how it is put together.

Wordless Messages from Mothers
Now that I've talked to you about what you should be saying to your children, there's more for you to think about. If you're a mother, I want to encourage you to think about the example you are setting. Are you a good example of healthy body image to them? Are you content with your age, or do you think you need to look like your daughter's sister? Is your lifestyle in balance? Do you talk negatively about your body around your children?

Your example will speak louder than your words. How you obsess about or neglect your body speaks volumes to them. Children need their mothers to model love and care for their own bodies. Your children will be aware if your main pursuit is beauty rather than character, and it will impact them negatively.

How Can I Help My Overweight Child?

Almost without exception, the compulsive overeaters I deal with replay messages in their heads from their moms. Do you remember Christine from chapter one? She's the one who is overweight but has a healthy body image now. Christine remembered shopping for clothes as the most humiliating side effect of being overweight as a child because of comments her mother made about her body in public. Christine's mom was usually frustrated because it was so hard to find half sizes and the prices were higher when she did locate them. Instead of a fun and exciting adventure, shopping was a humiliating and agonizing affair.

When I lost my leg in a farming accident, I didn't want to live. Now I like to play jokes with my leg, and I realize that I'm special and unique.

"That doesn't fit either? Honestly, Christine, I don't know what we are going to do!" her mother would yell loud enough for the whole dressing room to hear. On one fruitless trip, her mom tried a new store. She walked in with Christine by her side and queried in a voice that everyone in the store could hear, "Do you carry half sizes?" The distracted saleslady asked her to repeat. "You know, half sizes to fit her." Christine's mom pointed to her and everyone in line turned to look. "No," the saleslady answered. And Christine confirmed her belief that she was a fat, worthless nobody as they plunged on to the next store.

Christine's mom had good reason to be concerned about her over-weight child. Overweight children have increased health problems. It's not wrong to want the best for your children and want them not to face the social stigmas of being overweight. However, I advise parents of overweight children not to put them on a diet (unless there is a specific medical reason), but instead to make changes within the whole family system.

In dealing with your overweight child, the foundation of all your thoughts, actions, and words toward your child must be love, respect, and acceptance. Your child needs to know that you love her no matter what! Your love and approval should not be based on your child's body size. If your child is overweight, she is most likely experiencing some rejection by peers and even herself. This is why she needs your love and support all the more.

There are some important steps you can take to help your child.

1. Don't single out your child. You need to change the whole family's diet, but don't announce that it is because of your overweight child. Robin and Don adopted two children from Russia. The girls were only six months apart in age. Robin and Don had a very active lifestyle and they ate out almost every night. The restaurant food was fine for one of their daughters and did not cause her to gain weight, but it was different for the older one. Robin and Don had to make some major changes if they were going to help their daughter have a healthy body. Both hated to cook, so they alternated weeks to cook at home. They got a diet from the American Heart Association and started to feed the family more healthfully. It was a difficult decision, but they were very successful in not saying that this was all because of one daughter. In the end, the changes benefited the health of the entire family.

2. Be active as a family. Another change Robin and Don made was to plan family fun that included physical activity. They took walks and rode bikes after dinner. The children were exercising, and they didn't even know it. They signed the children up for dance lessons, and fostered their enjoyment of soccer and swim team. The older daughter decided to quit dance after two years, and Robin and Don allowed this. They didn't want to force her to do an activity that she didn't enjoy, but they also made sure she was not watching TV and playing video games all the time.

3. Teach your family healthy eating habits. We have so much to teach our children as they are growing. We teach them important spiritual truths about salvation. We teach them to make their beds and brush their teeth. We teach them not to lie or steal. We also need to teach them how to eat properly. If we leave it up to their natural cravings alone, they won't have healthy bodies.

Our new puppy Aggie is a great example. We give him a balanced and very expensive form of dog food that will supply him with the energy he needs to meet his every physical challenge. We put his dog food out for him every morning, but he waits to see if any crumb will fall from the breakfast table before he will touch his dog food. He finally eats it as a last-ditch effort when there's no hope of getting anything else. He doesn't understand how bad our food is for his digestive system. He just knows it tastes good and he wants it.

Our children aren't much different. We need to teach them how to eat properly. We need to serve well-balanced meals and explain why we have chosen the foods we serve. We need to teach them how large a serving to take, how many pieces of pizza to eat, and so on. My mom was a home economics major. Every meal that she put on the table contained the major food groups. I learned how to plan for and eat a well-balanced diet by example more than by words.

You can involve your children in planning, shopping for, and preparing meals. Eat together as a family as often as you can. There is nothing I enjoy more than sitting down with my husband and two children at the dinner table. It's a time for connecting and talking about the events of the day in a less hectic setting. If having dinner together is impossible due to work, school, or lesson schedules, perhaps you can make breakfast your family meal of the day. It may take sacrifice, effort, and planning, but you can make it happen if it is important to you.

---

*It's hard to face the fact that I just don't
look the way I used to look.*

Don't ever become the food gestapo. Don't forbid sweets and treats, but teach your children to enjoy these occasionally (Proverbs 25:16). Have good options available to them, and allow them to choose what to eat out of these options. It's wise to limit snacks to certain times of the day or a certain number each day. Teach your children to eat slowly. People who inhale their food don't have a chance to tune in to their bodies' signals to know whether they are getting full or not.

Let Your Voice Be Known
There is a great need for women to join together and let advertisers know how their influence is hurting women. As we have seen through this study, unhealthy body image develops from a combination of many factors. One such factor is definitely the effect of media and advertising.

Dr. Margo Maine in her book *Body Wars: An Activist's Guide,* encourages women and men to take a stand against the dehumanization of women's bodies in the culture we live in. She writes: "As we enter a new millennium, we must transform our society into one where women and their bodies will be respected and nurtured instead of abused and neglected. We have been talking about the problem long enough; we must move into action." Her book provides "ideas, action plans, strategies, and tactics to do just that."[1] Her book is a great resource for anyone who desires to become an activist for respect of women's bodies in the media.

Even if you choose not to let your voice be known in the media, you do have a voice in the world of influence that you live in.

Be the Voice of Reason

In the introduction I said that I felt called by God to write this book. I am so disheartened by the vile and ugly things women say and think about their bodies. I've spent the time researching and writing this book to help women stop the downward spiral of self-hate. I can see what a waste of time it is to be plagued by that deep crease that formed right above your lip when there is so much more to this life that you will miss out on. I hope you are feeling the same way by now. I hope you are fed up with your own body torment and that you long to see other women and girls break free from this destructive and ugly habit.

> [1]The Spirit of the Sovereign Lord is on me, because the Lord has anointed me to preach good news to the poor. He has sent me to bind up the brokenhearted, to proclaim freedom for the captives and release from darkness for the prisoners, [2]to proclaim the year of the Lord's favor and the day of vengeance of our God, to comfort all who mourn, [3]and provide for those who grieve in Zion—to bestow on them a crown of beauty instead of ashes, the oil of gladness instead of mourning, and a garment of praise instead of a spirit of despair. They will be called oaks of righteousness, a planting of the Lord for the display of his splendor (Isaiah 61:1–3).

❧ Do you see your body and your whole self as a planting of the Lord for the display of His splendor?

❧ Can you think of ways that you can proclaim the good news to other women so they can be free from body hate? How?

❧ Do you feel that you are living in God's favor? Why?

✿ In what ways have you been comforted by God about your body hate?

✿ Do you wear a crown of beauty?

✿ Is your heart glad?

✿ Do you wear a garment of praise?

The Isaiah passage you just read describes what God wants to show us about our bodies. I know that Isaiah was speaking directly to the nation of Israel, which lived in captivity to the Babylonians at the time. The temple and city of Jerusalem lay in ruins. God anointed His prophet Isaiah to proclaim His love and care for Israel in spite of their circumstances.

These words also describe the spiritual freedom God wants to bring to us. When we are body haters, we exist without the sense of God's favor. If you cannot look in the mirror right now and proclaim, "I have God's favor in the body I live in, without losing five pounds or straightening my teeth. I am completely favored by God," then you are not living in God's favor.

God wants to heal the damage your body hate has done to your life. He alone can provide the confidence and strength that is necessary to battle the comments and pressures that are all around you. God wants to comfort you and bandage your broken heart, release you from the captivity of rejecting your body, and proclaim His favor over you. You will know that you have received this from God when you find yourself wearing a crown of beauty. Do you see yourself as God's daughter—His princess? Do you recognize that your beauty is in wearing the image of God, not in having a buff body?

God wants to anoint you with the oil of gladness. Is your life full of gladness, or mourning? There is a time for weeping. Jesus Himself wept (John 11:35). Are you mourning about legitimate issues? Or are you mourning over your wrinkles, layers of fat, and ugly clothes?

When you are living in the reality of God's favor, your heart will be glad. You will be glad when you become conscious of your body. You will be glad when you observe women with better figures. Your gladness radiates the unique and special creation that you are.

My mom always complained about how flyaway and straight my hair was. I still hate my hair and feel like I can't do anything with it.

Your countenance will become a spirit of praise. It will be like a garment that you wear. For too long your face has revealed the despair you feel about how you look. Receiving God's favor will change all that. You will become radiant in the praise you feel for your God and the way He made you.

You will become a voice of reason in the circles in which you associate. You may not be called to write a Bible study about body image or speak publicly on this subject. You will have opportunities to speak to your children, your neighbors, your coworkers, your circle of friends. You can be a voice of reason when you see women succumbing to disparaging remarks about their bodies. You can encourage, pray for, and love other women, as God has loved you.

Your Work and God's Work

One of the most difficult spiritual journeys for me is to let God do His part, while I keep focused on my part. Whatever God commands in His Word, He never asks us to do on our own. He simply asks us to be willing to let Him work through us. This is true in forgiveness, loving others, prayer, and even receiving a healthy body image. Daniel is a great example of how to let God be God.

In the following verses from Daniel 1, underline what Daniel did (the verbs that describe Daniel's actions). Circle the things that God did.

But Daniel resolved not to defile himself with the royal food and wine, and he asked the chief official for permission not to defile himself this way (Daniel 1:8).

Now God had caused the official to show favor and sympathy to Daniel (Daniel 1:9).

To these four young men God gave knowledge and understanding of all kinds of literature and learning. And Daniel could understand visions and dreams of all kinds (Daniel 1:17).

And Daniel remained there until the first year of King Cyrus (Daniel 1:21).

In these scriptures Daniel resolved to follow God, ask the official for permission to eat certain foods, and remain where God had placed him. God caused the official to show favor to Daniel, and it was God who granted the knowledge and ability to understand visions.

Like Daniel, our part is to resolve in our hearts to follow God, take actions consistent with that decision, and remain where God has placed us. God is the one who gives us favor with others, and gives us the wisdom, knowledge, and gifts that we need to fulfill the tasks He gives us.

Here is one closing thought about our bodies from God's Word.

> [1]Now we know that if the earthly tent we live in is destroyed, we have a building from God, an eternal house in heaven, not built by human hands. [2]Meanwhile we groan, longing to be clothed with our heavenly dwelling, [3]because when we are clothed, we will not be found naked. [4]For while we are in this tent, we groan and are burdened, because we do not wish to be unclothed but to be clothed with our heavenly dwelling, so that what is mortal may be swallowed up by life. [5]Now it is God who has made us for this very purpose and has given us the Spirit as a deposit, guaranteeing what is to come. [6]Therefore we are always

confident and know that as long as we are at home in the body we are away from the Lord. [7]We live by faith, not by sight. [8]We are confident, I say, and would prefer to be away from the body and at home with the Lord. [9]So we make it our goal to please him, whether we are at home in the body or away from it. [10]For we must all appear before the judgment seat of Christ, that each one may receive what is due him for the things done while in the body, whether good or bad (2 Corinthians 5:1–10).

My prayer for you is that you will grow closer to God year by year. In that intimacy with God, I pray that you will discover the rich beauty that He created in you. I pray that you will exhibit that beauty to the people in your world, and that they would want to know God the way you do. I pray God's richest blessings over your life, and that you will give God praise because indeed you are beautiful!

Discussion Questions

1. How can you make a difference in other people's body hate?

2. How did your mom influence your body image?

3. What kinds of messages have you given as a mom or received from your mom?

4. How has your body image changed as a result of this study?

5. How has your relationship with God grown as a result of this study?

6. Go around the room and share one character quality that you appreciate about each person in your group. When your character qualities are shared, write them down on a piece of paper and keep it to remind you of your inner beauty.

7. Close by praying for group members as each journeys with God to a truer sense of herself and her true beauty.

Practical Makeover Tips

In chapter nine, I suggested you read this appendix for practical application to the issues we've been discussing. I hope this information is a helpful guide as you make important decisions about caring for your body.

Make Over Your Clothes

Beth began to face the facts. She had spent way too much time, money, and effort on her body. She would never have imagined it before, but when she tallied up her receipts for the year, she discovered that she had spent 25 percent of the family income on clothes, most of them for herself. Ron Blue recommends that your family budget include 3 to 4 percent for clothing.[1] Something definitely needed to change.

For Beth, clothing was a very significant issue. What about you? You should have the right kind of clothes for the social gatherings you attend. There may be times that you'll spend extra money on a special outfit. But ultimately, do you worship God or worship your clothes?

My daughter has learned how to get me to buy something for her—she searches the paper for sales. It is important for me to make sure I get a good bargain on the clothes I buy. I think it could be something in the female chromosome that makes women love to get a bargain. It is also a way for me to be a good steward of the money God has entrusted to me. I have many friends who like sales but who wouldn't sacrifice quality in their clothes for a good price. I think that is right for them. The most important thing is that your clothing expenditures are in balance.

Joan's closet looked like that of a schoolgirl who had to wear uniforms. Her uniform was dark-colored sweats. Her whole closet was full of navy and black. She thought she was too fat to wear color. Growth for Joan was going out and buying a new colorful outfit that fit her at just the size she was right then. She needed to value herself enough to wear nice clothes.

Take inventory of your closet. In which direction do you need to change? Is God speaking to you about your dedication to clothes? Could you go three months without making a clothing purchase for yourself? Or do you, like Joan, need to pay a little more attention to your wardrobe?

Make Over Your Makeup

Some women choose not to wear makeup as part of their spiritual discipline. They interpret certain scriptures as restricting makeup for women. To wear makeup for them would be to disobey God's Word. I encourage those women to be faithful to their understanding of Scripture and to do so with joy and gladness. God wants your obedience to be out of love for Him and not from a resentful heart. Your makeup is the beauty of an obedient and loving heart.

For the women who do not interpret Scripture to forbid makeup, I encourage you to wear it wisely. It's not a bad thing to have a makeover at a department store or elsewhere to learn how to apply makeup tastefully. However, be careful that you aren't deceived into thinking you need every product in your makeover. The salesperson's goal is to make you think you need a lot of products to be beautiful because that means more profits for the store.

It is not mandatory for women to wear makeup. If you wear it, make sure that it is not too time consuming and doesn't interfere with your budget. I use my makeup to protect my skin from the sun. It takes me about five minutes to apply all my makeup. I am a pretty efficient person, but I don't think it should take you more than about 15 minutes to put on your makeup each morning. If it takes you longer than 15 minutes, think about steps you can eliminate in your makeup process. You may be wearing too much makeup, or be too focused on looking just right.

Beth found she could make a few changes in her makeup. She learned that she could buy a cheaper brand, rather than the department store brand, and get the same results. (Some department store brands also produce a cheaper line. For instance, Lancôme also makes L'Oréal.) She continued to use a few of her favorite things, but got by with eye shadow and mascara from the drug store.

Joan has never worn much makeup because she didn't want to bother with it. She decided it would be appropriate to protect her skin from sun exposure, so she bought a foundation with sunscreen. She has some blush, eye shadow, and lipstick that she uses for special occasions, but for the most part she feels comfortable wearing minimal makeup each day.

Make Over Your Skincare

Skincare products are a major economic industry in America. There are tons of products that promise to cure whatever bothers you. It is wise to make a habit of cleaning and moisturizing your skin daily. Don't go for the most expensive products or be deceived by every promise. Experiment until you find a regimen that works for you, your time, and your budget. Use products that help protect your skin from sun damage and that heal your skin. Beth showed Joan how to care for her skin. They are both using the same product line and their skin looks fresh and healthy.

Make Over Your Diet

Okay, I know you hear your mother's voice, or another voice, telling you that you can't eat what you like anymore. Most Americans do eat horribly!

Are you one of them? I bet I could give you a Bible quiz and a food quiz and most of you would score higher on the food quiz. The American culture has been indoctrinated in how to eat right. We know which foods to avoid and which to eat lots of, but we don't make the right choices. Why?

There are several reasons. At the same time that we are being indoctrinated about what we *should* eat, we are being bombarded with what we *can* eat. We can find pizza, ice cream, french fries, doughnuts, and pastries on every street corner. It tastes good, it's available, and you don't have to think much about it. It is an easy way to make yourself happy, if just for a moment. A great deal of our eating is mindlessly pursuing quick fixes.

We establish bad habits that aren't easy to break. It takes discipline to eat right. You must make unpopular choices at restaurants. Others accuse you of making them feel guilty if you pass up dessert. No one likes to deny herself. Carefully considering what you eat and trying to eat food that is good for your body often goes against your natural cravings.

From the first hours after your birth, you learned to equate food with getting your needs met. A newborn's world is centered on eating and sleeping. If the newborn is receiving adequate nourishment, she will sleep and grow better. It is easy to equate food with feeling better, even when the food makes you feel guilty and sluggish after it is consumed.

If you are overweight, I counsel you not to begin a diet. Don't abuse your body through dieting and exercise regimens. Think about what your body needs when you make food and exercise decisions. Most obesity in women is the result of a poor body image. Make peace with the body you have right now at the weight you are. Establish in your mind that God loves and accepts you just the way you are, even if you gain 100 pounds. When you accept yourself, you are free to decide how to feed and nourish your body. When you honor and appreciate your body, you will not abuse it through overeating or with fad diets.

Food Is Important in God's Plan
God went to extreme measures to create a world for Adam and Eve to live in. A big part of that was planting trees in the garden that were good

for food and pleasing to the eye (Genesis 2:9). God told Adam in Genesis 2:16–17 that he was free to eat from any tree in the garden except the tree of the knowledge of good and evil. It is necessary to eat. It is fine to eat what you like. God created food to provide the nutrition that our bodies need for fuel, and He also created food for pleasure.

> If you find honey, eat just enough—too much of it, and
> you will vomit (Proverbs 25:16).

❧ Is it good to eat food that has little nutritional value?

❧ What makes it good to eat something like honey, something you eat almost purely for pleasure?

❧ Did God create food to give us pleasure?

Before and after the Fall it is clear that God intended food for both nourishment and pleasure. Jesus ate with His disciples and served them bread and fish after His resurrection (John 21:13). He longs to give us the right to eat of the tree of life (Revelation 22:14) where we can enjoy the wedding supper of the Lamb (Revelation 19:9). So how does food move so far from being an enjoyable experience to being the worst enemy or best friend of some?

Food, just like every other aspect of our existence on earth, was transformed after the Fall. Food became a major factor in the consequences of the curse, since food would be difficult to cultivate because of thorns and thistles. Today researchers and food specialists have solved these production problems in some parts of the world. Yet overabundance of food creates a whole new set of problems: overindulgence—using food to solve emotional problems. The curse still plagues us today. In America we are tormented with too many food choices.

The majority of women reading this book may have a legitimate need to lose weight. This is not a weight-loss book, so you may wish to receive more specific guidance from a dietitian. When you have peace with your body, you will naturally want to treat your body well. Some women are uneducated about nutrition. Many would be surprised to find ways to prepare food and enjoy it while consuming more vitamins and minerals, fewer empty calories, and less fat.

Many women struggle to eat correctly because they have an unrealistic target weight in mind. It is not wise to go on a diet to lose a certain number of pounds. I recommend that women learn what their bodies should weigh in order to be healthy, then learn how to eat and exercise to get there—even if it takes years to achieve the goal weight. One tool you can use to determine your healthy range of body weight is to use the Body Mass Index (BMI).

Here is a three-step process to determine your BMI.

1. Multiply your weight in pounds by 703.
2. Square your height in inches.
3. Divide the total from step 1 by the total of step 2. The answer is your BMI.

Marybeth's BMI is 24.2.

1. She weighs 150 pounds x 703 = 105,450.
2. She is 66 inches tall squared = 4356.
3. 105,450 divided by 4356 = 24.2 BMI.

An adult woman's BMI should be between 20 and 27.3 to be in the healthy range.

If that is too complicated, you can consult with your physician or dietitian to determine what is a healthy weight for you.

Suggested Eating Plan

If you are deciding to eat better, I recommend that you choose a food plan that allows you to eat normal food from the grocery store and make real-life decisions in restaurants. Many people are successful at losing weight on special and bizarre diets, but they do not keep the weight off. Many of these diets abuse the body.

The only right motivation for changing your diet is to treat your body right, not to look better for your 20th high-school reunion.

Don't make dietary changes that may help you lose weight but are harmful to you.

Good Eaters Take Notice

There are people who exhibit an eating disorder that isn't noticed by their doctors or even friends. Some women eat so perfectly that their blood work reveals a completely healthy specimen, yet their spirits are not free. These women are overcommitted to fitness and wellness to the exclusion of spiritual well-being. Do you place your trust in your good eating and exercise, and not in God's provision and care for you? If so, you may need to work a little more on your eating habits as well. You should be free to have a piece of birthday cake or other dessert.

Here are some suggestions to establish healthy eating patterns:

1. Schedule three meals a day at regular times.
2. Try to eat with your family at the kitchen table as often as possible. If you are single, invite others to eat with you at your kitchen table.
3. Don't nibble during meal preparation.
4. When you eat, concentrate on experiencing your food, its texture, smell, and taste, and not shoveling everything into your mouth.
5. Eat slowly; put your fork down between bites.
6. Drink half your body weight in ounces of fresh water daily. For example, if you weigh 120 pounds, you should drink 60 ounces of water each day.
7. Enjoy pleasant music and conversation during your meals.
8. Recognize that it is normal to feel full after a meal and your belt or waistband will feel a little tighter. Don't condemn yourself for eating and enjoying your meal.
9. Don't keep a record of forbidden foods. You should include desserts and foods you like (in proper proportion) in your regular eating schedule.
10. Don't eat in the car, bus, bedroom, or bathroom, or on the run.
11. Don't try to lose weight too fast. Losing one-half pound a week is healthier for your body.

12. Eat fewer fatty foods and simple sugars.
13. Eat more fresh fruits, vegetables, and whole grains.
14. Engage in moderate physical activity.

Make Over Your Exercise

Do you feel another lecture coming on? Yes, we all need to exercise. Americans are too sedentary. One thing I want to make clear to you: I hate to exercise. In spite of that fact, I have been exercising three times a week since 1995.

Some people find that after committing to exercise, they start to like it. Not me. I hate sweating. I can't wait to finish. I love to check it off my list. I never throw in an extra day just for good health.

I do love what having an exercise program does for me, though. It has lowered my blood cholesterol. It makes me stronger and helps me sleep better. I believe that I have firmer muscles in my thighs in my forties than at any other time in my life. I commit to exercise because I know it is a part of treating my body well.

I recommend that you start out with an exercise commitment that is not too strenuous. You could choose to walk around the block three times a week, then build up to walking three times a week for 30 minutes. Eventually, build up to walking fast enough to keep your heart beating at your target heart rate for aerobic fitness for 30 minutes.

Make Over Your Shopping Habits

I've already mentioned making over your clothes habit. Much of over-indulgence in clothes and food starts while shopping. In fact, you may find as you get your eating and clothing under control you have more money to use for eternal purposes.

Establishing a budget for your total household expenses is mandatory for managing God's money well. Even if you can't get your husband to support you in your effort to make a household budget, you can make a budget for the spending you do. Decide what is the right amount of money to spend on clothes and food, including eating out.

Next, you can make over your shopping habits by making lists.

Most of us do this when we shop for food, but it is also very helpful when shopping for clothes. Before you go shopping, go through the clothes you have. Decide what you need and think about what you are looking for. When you shop, don't be distracted by everything you see, but have specific clothing needs in mind. It's okay to splurge occasionally, but it shouldn't be a regular occurrence.

When shopping for food, do the same. Don't buy items that aren't on your shopping list.

I hope you learned some ways to care for your body from the other women in your group. Wanting to take care of your body to glorify God brings true freedom and balance.

Help for Those with Deeper Issues

This study may have made you realize just how much poor body image has affected your life. As you have probably noticed, it's rare to find anyone who doesn't think that something is unattractive about her body. This is a common problem. But there are problems associated with poor body image that need more help and attention than this book and a study group can provide. Of course, not everyone has developed addictions and destructive behaviors due to a poor body image, but don't feel discouraged if you have. Do get help for yourself and those you love. Though these are deeper problems, they are not unsolvable problems.

Eating Disorders

Compulsive Overeating

Women who find themselves addicted to food feel that they are moral failures. They have a sense that if they had more self-discipline this problem would instantly go away. They are ashamed to get help and many times don't feel that they deserve help.

Help is available. Maybe you feel that you've tried everything and there is just something different about you. That is not true. Jeremiah 29:11–14 promises that God has a plan for you and that you will find it when you search for Him with all your heart. God does want you to learn how to turn your addiction to food into dependence on Him. Women have overcome their addiction to food in a variety of ways. It is not the tool (Weight Watchers, First Place, etc.), it is the relationship with God that makes the biggest difference. Don't give up! Seek guidance and counsel.

Confess your desire to stop your addiction to a spiritual person who can give you support and a professional who can help you unlock the door to your food addiction. Doing this body image Bible study is a great foundation for overcoming the dependence you have on food. I hope you have come to accept your body a little more through the things you have written, what you have read, and the love and acceptance you have experienced from your group and God.

Do not seek out help with an eating plan *to lose weight!* Do seek out help with an eating plan *to take care of your body.* Eat healthfully out of gratefulness and appreciation for the gift of your body. Do it to take care of yourself, not to make yourself look better on the outside. It is good to have a bottom-line weight, a weight you won't go under, but don't have a goal weight that says "I am suitable to present to the world since I weigh this now!" In fact, it would be great if you threw out the scales and evaluated the results of your eating plan by how you feel (the energy you have) and how your clothes fit.

Anorexia/Bulimia

Just as in the case of compulsive overeating, anorexia (compulsive restricting) and bulimia (compulsive eating along with purging the food with laxatives, throwing up, compulsive exercising, or a combination of these) are addictive behaviors. You need the help of someone, a professional or a group, to stop these life-threatening and destructive behaviors. There are many facets to this problem. A negative body image is just one aspect of the problem. Food and eating habits are not the problem—they are the symptoms of the problem. You need to learn how to understand and accept yourself in order to stop the self-destructive behavior.

Helping Someone with an Eating Disorder

When you suspect your child or someone else you love has an eating disorder, you want to do something. God can use you to help that person get help. Often your natural instincts are to persuade them to eat more food. Some parents and loved ones even try to force the person to eat. This does little good. Here is a list of do's and don'ts that I share with parents when they are facing an eating disorder.

Don't
- get into power struggles over food
- offer pat answers
- impose guilt
- blame yourself

Do
- lovingly confront the symptoms you see
- get professional help for family members under legal age—encourage adults to get help
- get support for yourself
- learn about eating disorders
- require the person to take responsibility for herself/himself
- talk openly and honestly about your feelings
- give honest feedback about appearance
- recognize that the problem isn't just food
- listen
- show love and affection

Body Dysmorphic Disorder

This is a real and growing problem. It is characterized by delusional obsessions with imagined or slight physical imperfections. It can drive women to depression, suicide, or isolation from others. Experts believe that it is underdiagnosed. There is help, and if you suspect that you or your child are overreacting to physical characteristics, you should seek out professional help.

Considering Cosmetic Surgery

I do believe that there are appropriate reasons to have plastic surgery. I am glad that there are so many skilled physicians whom God can use in the healing process. Before you have plastic surgery, think about it, talk to people you respect who have sound, healthy advice, and consider the options available to you. It is not a sin to have plastic surgery, but it is important for you to think through this decision and recognize what your goals really are.

Most procedures require anesthesia. You need to fully understand the risks and consider whether they are worth taking in your particular case. In the majority of situations cosmetic surgery is not worth the risk and money required.

Depression

Depression is characterized by a change in sleep pattern, change in appetite, overwhelming feelings of worthlessness, lack of concentration, lack of motivation, loss of energy, agitation, restlessness, irritability, or thoughts of death or suicide. It is important that you recognize the symptoms of depression and seek out help. Depression can be treated. There are many causes of depression. It is possible to develop depression from constantly berating yourself and your body. If you have the symptoms listed above, please discuss them with your doctor or a Christian counselor.

Anxiety

Anxiety is characterized by intense worry, nervousness, panic attacks, and overwhelming fear of situations and circumstances. It can often lead to fear of leaving your home. As with depression, anxiety can be treated. You can overcome the panic and fear with the help of God, your doctor, and a Christian counselor.

Focus on the Family and New Life Clinics also have Christian referral resources if you need them. You can reach Focus on the Family at 1-800-A-FAMILY, and New Life Clinics at 1-877-652-5622 or 1-800-NEW-LIFE.

Tips for Group Leaders

Scripture says that when you desire to be a leader, you desire a good thing (1 Timothy 3:1). God has placed a desire in your heart to help women know Him and His Word better. This book was written as a tool to aid you and help your group grow. I encourage you to commit your group's study to God (Proverbs 16:3). I will give you suggestions and direction, but it is most important that you follow the leading of the Holy Spirit as you provide direction to the group.

Publicity

You may be leading this study with a group that is already in existence, such as a book club, Sunday school class, or support group. The only publicity needed is an announcement that includes the date that you will begin the study and instructions on how to purchase books. If your group meets in a home, you'll need to make these arrangements and include meeting times and dates in the publicity.

If you are publicizing this study in your church, you should discuss the best ways to do this with your church staff. They will have an idea of how far in advance to begin publicity and how to handle sign-up. If you are meeting at the church, you will want to follow their procedures for reserving a room for your meeting.

Preparing Your Heart

As you dedicate this study to God, you will be amazed at the ways He will direct you. He will give you the encouragement, guidance, and strength you need to help others follow Him. You will be blessed in your position of leadership even more than the women who attend your group. The greatest blessing will be from your intimate relationship with God. You will watch Him working in your life and giving you wisdom to share with those you minister to.

I recommend that you read and answer the questions from at least the first two chapters before you begin to lead the study. You may choose to read through the entire book ahead of time, if you wish. The other women will look to you for guidance, and it will be helpful if you have some familiarity with the book and its message.

Small groups of eight to 10 participants would be the ideal size for this type of discussion, but you may need to have a smaller or larger gathering based on your group's specific needs.

The reading material involves 10 weeks, but I suggest that you meet for 11 weeks if at all possible. When you meet for 11 weeks, it gives you the opportunity to have an introduction session that will set the tone for the rest of the study. I have found that it is helpful for individuals to know one another and have a sense of safety and fun in order for them to be open to the most productive sharing. This is why an introduction session can be foundational to setting the tone of your meetings. In the introduction session, you can introduce the book, yourself, and one another. In our busy world, many of us may see each other at church, yet know very little about each other. A suggested hour of introduction could go like this:

First Meeting Agenda

First 15 Minutes: This time is for arrival, a light snack, and informal talking. I suggest you have name tags unless the women know one another well.

Thirty Minutes: Call the group together and have a time of welcome, prayer, and introduction of the study. You could provide a handout that lists the dates and chapters that will be studied on each date. This is very helpful if you are skipping a week for spring break, for example, as someone who has to miss a meeting may feel lost and talk herself out of coming to the next meeting. If she can check her schedule, it will help her feel like she knows where the rest of the group is.

You can take care of the details of purchasing the book at this time, if participants are purchasing the book from you, or explain where to get a copy.

Share your personal goals and hopes for the next 10 weeks; help the women see what you are hoping to accomplish in this study. Your goal may be that the women will get to know one another better and feel they have a friend in this group. Another goal is that each of you would be personally changed by the study of God's Word. If you desire, you could share your own testimony of what you have learned so far by reading the book and doing the exercises.

Explain how the book is organized. There are questions within each chapter that would be most beneficial if the women answered them in their own journals. There isn't space in the book to write their answers, and the introduction suggests that they buy a notebook or journal in which they can keep their personal answers. We decided to publish the book this way so that readers would feel free to be totally honest with their answers without feeling that they are permanently placed in a book. It also gives them a chance to share the book with a friend or relative without fearing that personal feelings or opinions are being exposed. The women will get the most out of the book if they take the time to read the scriptures (which are included right in the text) and write out answers in their journals. They do not have to share anything from their journals in group time, but they may want to bring them to the meetings to make notes or to refer to if they do want to share from them.

Ground Rules

Go over the ground rules that are suggested in the introduction to the book. The purpose of this time is to help women feel comfortable sharing from their hearts. Your group may want to add other guidelines, but those have proven helpful in making women feel comfortable about what they share.

As you move to the get-acquainted exercise, explain that this is the only time that women are required to speak out and share information with the group. After this, it is optional. There are many shy women who might be intimidated by group sharing.

Get-Acquainted Exercise

You can make this time light and fun, or meaningful, depending on your group and how well they know one another.

Begin by having people share a little about themselves, where they are from, how long they have lived in the area, their family, their work, and so on. You could write these questions on a poster or simply ask them verbally.

Play a Game

Choose one of the following suggestions, or come up with an idea of your own.

1. Go around the room and ask each woman to share her most embarrassing moment. (This might not be the best exercise if there are some very shy or insecure women in the group.)

2. Have the women divide up into groups in certain parts of the room by revealing tidbits about themselves: For example, if you think there is a right way and a wrong way to put toilet paper on a roll, go to the left corner of the room; the others meet by the piano. Think of about six or seven of these. Laugh and discuss your findings about one another.

3. Give each woman a piece of paper and have her write two true statements about herself and one false. Tell her to be clever in what she writes because everyone is going to guess who the statements are about and which one is false. You want to try to fool everyone with the false statement. Make sure they don't put their names on the papers, but they have to "fess up" when you

play the game. An example would be: 1) I am from Florida. 2) I love to read fiction. 3) I have been suspected of robbery. (The first and last are true, and the second is false.) You will have a lot of fun hearing about the time she was suspected of robbery.

4. Make an acrostic on a large poster board with the letters of B-O-D-Y-I-M-A-G-E down the side. Ask women to come up and write the nicest word they can think of to describe women's bodies for each letter. For example, for the letter B, a woman could write "Beautiful."

5. Think of a fun get-acquainted game that you enjoyed at a party or fellowship recently and use it.

Meaningful Time

If you desire more meaningful time, you could give each woman a piece of paper and have her number from 1 to however many women are in the group. (For example, if there are 12 women, number from 1–12.) Then place your hand over the first person. Instruct her to place a dash after number 1, but ask the rest of the women to write the first positive word that comes to their minds when they think of this woman. Have them write that word beside number 1. Continue to do this around the circle, making sure the woman you have your hand over has placed a dash on her paper. After everyone is finished, have the ladies share the one word with the woman, one at a time. For instance, if Jane is number 1, have everyone go around the room and share the word they wrote for Jane after number 1. Be sure to include yourself in this exercise.

Even though all of these sound like a lot of fun, choose just one for this night. You will not have enough time to do them all.

Close in prayer and encourage everyone to read chapters one and two before next week's session.

Suggestions for Prayer

I encourage women to have some kind of prayer list during group Bible studies like this. There is a bond of intimacy that develops as you

pray for one another. Sometimes women use up too much time sharing details of prayer requests, and this leaves you without enough time
for study. One way you can avoid this is to have a sheet where each
person can write her prayer requests before the session. If you have
access to a copier during the session, you could make enough copies
for everyone to take home to pray. Another idea is to use e-mail to
share the requests with one another.

Leading the Group

I have included discussion questions at the end of each chapter. You
need to decide how you will use these in your group time. If you have
a very talkative group, you may not be able to use all six questions.
Choose three or four that you think are most helpful from the study
that week, then do the remainder if time permits. As I already mentioned, God will show you the best way to lead your group. You may
want to make up some of your own discussion questions. Some leaders will give a brief overview of the chapter before going into the discussion questions. Make sure that you spend time preparing your
heart and listening to God tell you how He wants you to lead.

You don't have to teach this material. Everyone has read the chapter, so if you do not feel gifted at teaching, don't try to teach. If you
have a gift for teaching, and feel it would be helpful to the women,
share your insights before discussion.

I hope that you will see yourself as a facilitator. You are there to
encourage discussion and learning. You can set the example by sharing first so others will follow, but don't do this every time. Don't be
afraid of silence. The biggest mistake leaders make is to get intimidated by silence. Silence doesn't mean that no one is getting anything
out of the study. If you don't experience times of silence, certain
women will never share. If you are particularly worried about silence,
try counting slowly to 10 in your head before jumping in to share or
moving on to the next question. Trust that God is at work in the
silence.

Be sensitive to the women in your group. If you have someone who is shy, she will need extra encouragement from you as she shares. If you have someone who is taking over the group, be sensitive to the others by recognizing that it is your job to make sure the group is helpful to everyone. You shouldn't be bashful about interrupting and redirecting the group if it is going in the wrong direction, or if someone is dominating the discussion. Most of the questions don't have right or wrong answers, but if anyone is sharing heresy or untruths about God's Word, you should kindly confront her.

Suggestions for Weeks Two through 11

These sessions will run about the same as your first session. You can better gauge how many of the discussion questions you can use each week by the first session. Do make sure that you are discussing issues that are important and helpful to the women. Don't let this become an empty time. This discussion time can be very powerful and encouraging in women's lives. It provides practical insights to make important changes. You may want to take some time in session 11 to bring closure to the study. Make sure you do discuss question number seven.

Endnotes

Introduction

1. Smith, James Bryan and Lynda Graybeal, *A Spiritual Formation Workbook* (HarperCollins: San Francisco, 1993) p.9.

Chapter 1

1. Kathleen Corcoran, "More Women Seeking Cosmetic Surgery," www.plasticsurgery.org/mediactr/webwomen.html.

2. ANRED Anorexia Nervosa and Related Eating Disorders, (http://www.anred.com).

3. Kimberly Shearer Palmer, "Colleges Start to Realize Men Need Body-image Help, Too," *USA Today,* May 10, 2001, 15A.

4. "The Prevalence of Eating Disorders." Located at http://www.edap.rg/edifo/stats.html.

5. "The Prevalence of Eating Disorders." Located at http://www.edap.rg/edifo/stats.html.

6. "Coaching the Coaches," *Psychology Today* (March/April 1992), p. 10.

7. "Searching for the Perfect Body." Found at http://people.aol.com/people/000904/magstories/index.html, posted August 25, 2000.

Chapter 2

1. Margo Maine, *Body Wars: An Activist's Guide* (Gurze Books: Carlsbad, CA, 2000), p. 210.

Chapter 3
1. Bruce Springsteen, "Better Days," Bruce Springsteen's Greatest Hits.

Chapter 5
1. Smith and Graybeal, p. 69.

2. Roger Reynolds, "Just As I Am Wellness Seminar," at The Cooper Institute for Aerobics Research, Dallas, Texas, October 15, 1998.

Chapter 6
1. "Researchers Discover Mind's Key to Self-Image." Located at www.aan.com/public/nrelease/05080, May 9, 2001.

2. Faye Angus, *Daily Guideposts*, 1993, (© by Daily Guideposts, 1992).

Chapter 7
1. Henry Gariepy, *Forty Days with the Savior* (Thomas Nelson, Nashville, 1995), pp. 92–93.

2. Flora Slosson Wuellner, *Prayer, Stress & Our Inner Wounds* (The Upper Room, Nashville, 1995), p. 50.

3. Flora Slosson Wuellner, "Transformation," *The Weavings Reader: Living with God in the World*, ed. by John Megabgab (The Upper Room, Nashville, 1993), p. 31.

Chapter 8
1. The Oprah Winfrey Show, "New Medical Tests," March 12, 2001.

2. Smith and Graybeal, p. 38.

Chapter 9
1. Located at http://www.bodytalkmagazine.com/mixedlolies.htm, July 20, 2001.

2. Symeon the New Theologian (A.D. 949–1022), Hymn 15. Located at www.christianrecovery.com/library/body.html.

Chapter 10
1. Margo Maine, p. x-xi.

Appendix I
2. Ron Blue, *Master Your Money* (Thomas Nelson: Nashville, 1991), p. 141.

FOCUS ON THE FAMILY®

Welcome to the Family!

Whether you received this book as a gift, borrowed it from
a friend, or purchased it yourself, we're glad you read it! It's just
one of the many helpful, insightful, and encouraging
resources produced by Focus on the Family.

In fact, that's what Focus on the Family is all about—providing inspira-
tion, information, and biblically based advice to people in all stages of life.

It began in 1977 with the vision of one man, Dr. James Dobson, a licensed
psychologist and author of 16 best-selling books on marriage, parenting,
and family. Alarmed by the societal, political, and economic pressures
that were threatening the existence of the American family, Dr. Dobson
founded Focus on the Family with one employee—an assistant—
and a once-a-week radio broadcast, aired on only 36 stations.

Now an international organization, Focus on the Family is dedicated
to preserving Judeo-Christian values and strengthening the family
through more than 70 different ministries, including eight separate
daily radio broadcasts; television public service announcements;
11 publications; and a steady series of books and award-winning
films and videos for people of all ages and interests.

Recognizing the needs of, as well as the sacrifices and important
contributions made by, such diverse groups as educators, physicians,
attorneys, crisis pregnancy center staff, and single parents,
Focus on the Family offers specific outreaches to uphold and
minister to these individuals, too. And it's all done for one purpose,
and one purpose only: to encourage and strengthen individuals
and families through the life-changing message of Jesus Christ.

• • •

For more information about the ministry, or if we can be of help to your
family, simply write to Focus on the Family, Colorado Springs, CO 80995
or call 1-800-A-FAMILY (1-800-232-6459). Friends in Canada may write
Focus on the Family, P.O. Box 9800, Stn. Terminal, Vancouver, B.C. V6B 4G3
or call 1-800-661-9800. Visit our Web site—www.family.org—
to learn more about Focus on the Family or to find out if
there is an associate office in your country.

We'd love to hear from you!

Soul Soothers
From Focus on the Family®

A Deep Drink of Spiritual Refreshment
Once children arrive, many Christian mothers get so caught up in caring for their families that they neglect nurturing their own souls. Avoid emptiness and burnout with the encouragement and direction found in Tender Mercy for a Mother's Soul. Filled with heartwarming illustrations and practical ideas for growing in a daily personal walk with Jesus—and written in an inviting, woman-to-woman style—this delightful hardcover will motivate even the busiest mom to care for her own soul and benefit from God's strength.

Reclaim Your God-Given Worth
Many women accept the world's messages about what we should be—young, beautiful, rich, successful. Others try to measure themselves by more traditional roles—submissive, gentle, hospitable. But what does the Bible say a woman should be? A Woman's Search for Worth explores this wide-ranging topic by looking at the wholeness available through a relationship with Christ. Become the beautiful, confident masterpiece you were destined to be as you discover your true identity in God!

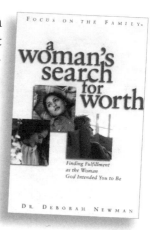

• • •

Look for these special books in your Christian bookstore or request a copy by calling 1-800-A-FAMILY (1-800-232-6459).
Friends in Canada may write Focus on the Family,
P.O. Box 9800, Stn. Terminal,
Vancouver, B.C. V6B 4G3 or call 1-800-661-9800.

Visit our Web site (www.family.org) to learn more about the ministry or find out if there is a Focus on the Family associate office in your country.